W9-ASW-062

REVISED EDITION

Dining In—Boston

COOKBOOK

REVISED EDITION

Dining In—Boston

COOKBOOK

A Collection of Gourmet Recipes for Complete Meals
from the Boston Area's Finest Restaurants

STEVEN RAICHLEN

Foreword by
DICK SYATT

PEANUT BUTTER
PUBLISHING

Peanut Butter Publishing
Mercer Island, Washington

GROVE HALL

MAR 87

TITLES IN SERIES

Special thanks to Linda Wong and Barbara Sause
who helped research the manuscript.

Cover photograph by Kenneth Redding
Edited by Charles Malody
Production by April Ryan
Illustrations by Carol Naumann
Typesetting by April Ryan

Copyright © 1983 by Peanut Butter Publishing
2445 76th Avenue S.E., Mercer Island, WA 98040 (206) 236-1982
All rights reserved. Printed in the United States of America
Revised Edition November 1983

ISBN 0-89716-124-6

DEDICATION

This book is dedicated

to my Parents,

who introduced me to

the pleasure of dining out.

CONTENTS

FOREWORD

There are some people who eat to live and others, who live to eat. I am proud to include myself in the catagory of the latter. Indeed, my New Year's resolution last year was to eat out more and feel less guilty about the expense and calories. Not surprisingly, this is one New Year's resolution I have had no problem keeping!

Between you and me, I love the entire experience of dining out ... the ritual of being led to your table and seated, of perusing the menu, of letting the waiter know that I mean business when it comes to eating. I am the sort of person who does not so much eat his food as make love to it, and at the end of the meal, I am not embarassed about loosening my belt a notch or two, and waddling out to my car.

Steven Raichlen and I share the same enthusiasm for the dining out experience. That is why I enjoy his restaurant reviews in *Boston Magazine* so much, and I look forward to having him as a guest on my radio show. Steve and I have actually reviewed several restaurants together—watch out, there is nothing worse than having two restaurant critics at the same table!

Boston has scores of great restaurants, and this book covers 21 of the best. For the restaurant goer, Steven Raichlen has included a full report on the food, setting, and service. And for the practicing cook, as well as the armchair epicure, he presents mouth-watering recipes for some of the tastiest dishes in Boston.

Therefore, I believe that *Dining In—Boston* will be an invaluable tool for your dining pleasure. And please, do yourself and the rest of us a favor: Let the maitre d' or chef know if you are happy or unhappy with your meal and service.

Bon Appetit!

Dick Syatt

PREFACE

When I first moved to Boston, I was warned that if I wanted to eat well, I would have to learn how to cook for myself. Implied by the advice, I suppose, was that Boston was not a dine-out city, at least not one with the variety and stature of my previous domicile—Paris. As I had come to New England to teach cooking classes, I was not particularly worried by the warning.

It was not long, however, before I began to discover just the contrary—that Boston's restaurants had a lot to offer, and not just to a cooking teacher who, from time to time, tired of this own cooking. There is great seafood in Boston—a bounty found in few other American cities—suppied by the fish-rich waters of the North Atlantic. There is also, in this oldest of American cities, a long and continuous tradition of fine dining, including a handful of restaurants that opened their doors to the public more than a century ago. I soon came to meet the many faces of ethnic Boston, whose Oriental, Italian and Slavic communities dish up their exotic specialties in marvelous profusion. I arrived in this city of gold domes and tall church spires just in time to witness the birth of a veritable culinary revolution, led by bright young chefs who drew their inspiration from French nouvelle cuisine and their ingredients from the comestible cornucopia of New England.

The research and writing of *Dining In–Boston* has been an adventure of culinary discovery for me. What better way to learn about cooking than to meet and talk to the chefs of Boston's twenty-one top restaurants? These remarkable cooks have generously shared not only their prized recipes, but also their hard-earned kitchen wisdom. It is with great pleasure and excitement that I pass on the secrets of their specialties to the readers of *Dining In–Boston*.

"A recipe is like a score of music," remarked one of the chefs I interviewed. I think the analogy is worth pursuing. Anyone with the barest musical training can hammer out note by note the score of a Brandenburg concerto. Let a true musician bring but a little sensitivity, improvisation and feeling to the piece, and the audience will weep for joy when it hears the performance. So it is with cooking. A teaspoon by teaspoon rendition of a recipe never produced a culinary masterpiece. Add a dash of inspiration, a pinch of folly, a splash of love to the recipes in *Dining In–Boston*—as do the chefs who prepare these dishes in their restaurants—and you will wind up with food that makes beautiful music.

Discover the taste of Boston, then, with the talented men and women chefs who make it possible. From all of us, happy cooking. And, *bien sûr, bon appetit!*

Steven Raichlen

Allegro

Dinner for Six

Peperoni Arrosti

Fettuccine con Panna

Pesce Spada alla Griglia con Salsa Verde

Zucchini Trifolati

Zuccotto

Wines:

With the Fettuccine—Lugana, Salvalai, 1978

With the Swordfish—Meursault Poruzots, Ropiteau, 1976

James Burke and Bonnie Goodson, Proprietors and Chefs

"It wasn't easy opening a Northern Italian restaurant in this area," recall Lillian and David Coltin, the youthful founders of Allegro in Waltham. Expecting the enormous servings awash in tomato sauce typical of most Anglo-Italian restaurants, the public was at first mystified by the delicacy and sophistication of Allegro's offerings. Some people, accustomed to filling up on a single dish, complained that the portions of Allegro's carefully balanced six course meals were too small. "That's simply not Northern Italian cooking," said the Coltins who had gradually trained their clients to accord Allegro's fare the respect once reserved exclusively for French haute cuisine.

New owners Jim Burke, formerly of The Harvest, and Bonnie Goodson purchased the restaurant in 1981 and have continued the Northern Italian bill of fare with its beguiling simplicity and flavors. The dining room has remained much as it was with its high tech lights, exposed brick, and Italian travel posters. Meats and fish are still cooked to perfection on a grill. The new owners carry forth the convictions of the restaurant's founders that "Our food did the talking for us, so we kept the decor and service as simple as possible; Allegro means 'joyful, pleasant, enjoyable' in Italian, and that's what restaurant dining should be."

458 Moody Street
Waltham
891-5486

PEPERONI ARROSTI
Fresh-Roasted Peppers with an Aromatic Vinaigrette

6 medium-size red, yellow,
     and green sweet peppers
salt
VINAIGRETTE SAUCE

1 tablespoon oregano
2 tablespoons capers,
     well rinsed
4 cloves garlic, peeled
     and bruised

1. Preheat the broiler for 15 minutes.
2. Cut each pepper in half lengthwise and remove stems, seeds, and core. Flatten the peppers to expose as much skin surface as possible and arrange by color on baking sheets. (The different types of peppers will cook at different rates).
3. Reduce broiler temperature, if possible, and place the peppers under the flame until the skin puffs and chars. Peel off as much skin as possible with your fingers, then trim off any remaining skin with a paring knife.
4. Choose a deep, flat dish in which the peppers can be presented at the table. Place a layer of peppers in the dish, alternating rows of red, green, and yellow. Sprinkle lightly with salt. Spoon some Vinaigrette Sauce over the peppers and top with oregano, capers, and garlic. Repeat this proceedure with another layer of peppers and Vinaigrette Sauce. Marinate for at least 6 hours before serving.

Note: This dish can be prepared ahead of time, but remove the garlic cloves after 6 hours to avoid a bitter taste.

Red peppers are at their best in October, when they are heavy and fleshy. The roasting brings out their sweetness and makes them easier to peel.

VINAIGRETTE SAUCE

¼ cup red wine vinegar
½ teaspoon salt

1 anchovy fillet
1 cup olive oil

Whirl the wine vinegar, salt, and anchovy in a blender. Gradually dribble in the olive oil and mix well.

The most important thing in all these recipes is being able to distinguish between medicre ingredients and top quality ingredients. If you don't go to the trouble of finding good peppers or swordfish, the results just won't be the same.

FETTUCCINE CON PANNA
Homemade Noodles with Cream and Cheese

2½ cups all-purpose flour
½ cup semolina
    salt
4 large eggs, plus
    1 extra yolk
1 tablespoon olive oil

1½ cups whipping cream
½ cup plus 2 tablespoons
    unsalted butter
    freshly ground black pepper
1¼ cups freshly grated Parmi-
    giano Reggiano cheese

1. Combine the flour, semolina, and a pinch of salt in the bowl of a sturdy electric mixer. Stop the machine and make a depression in the center of the dry ingredients with your hand. Mix the eggs, yolks, and olive oil in a separate bowl and pour into the center of the dry ingredients. Start the machine again and mix on the lowest speed. Transfer the dough onto a floured surface and knead for 10 minutes with the heel of your palm.

2. Divide the pasta dough into four equal parts and keep covered with a clean dish cloth. Set a pasta machine to its widest setting. Pass each of the four balls of dough through the rollers eight times, folding the dough in half each time.

3. Close the rollers to the next setting and feed the dough through without folding. Continue changing the roller setting until the dough is paper thin, about 1/32 inch.

4. Dry the sheets of dough on towels for about 20 minutes; they should cut cleanly into 10-inch sections. Feed the sheets of dough through the machine's fettuccine cutters and leave the pasta to dry on a towel until ready to use.

5. To cook the pasta, bring 4 gallons of water and 1 tablespoon of salt to a rolling boil. Add the fresh fettuccine and cook for 3 to 4 minutes. Do not overcook; drain the fettuccine and do not rinse.

6. Meanwhile, combine the cream and butter in a 12-inch skillet and cook over medium heat for 5 minutes or until the mixture thickens slightly.

7. Add the cooked fettuccine, salt and pepper, and the grated cheese to the simmering cream sauce. Stir over medium-low heat until the cheese dissolves and thickens the cream. The noodles should be thoroughly coated. Serve in soup bowls with extra black pepper and grated cheese on the side.

Note: Semolina is a high protein durhum wheat flour. Its high gluten content helps the noodles hold their shape. Semolina can be purchased in most Italian groceries and health food stores.

Our pasta, dried, tastes better than most I've sampled fresh. That's because we use only eggs, olive oil, flour, and semolina. There's no water in the dough at all. We cook our pasta in individual saucepans at the restaurant, not in a single pot of boiling water which gets gummy and starchy during the course of the evening. We cook the sauce for the pasta in individual saucepans, too.

PESCE SPADA ALLA GRIGLIA CON SALSA VERDE
Grilled Swordfish with a Tart Green Sauce

1 cup olive oil
⅓ cup fresh lemon juice
salt

6 (½-pound) swordfish
steaks
SALSA VERDE

1. Combine the olive oil, lemon juice, and salt to taste. Marinate the fish in the mixture for 30 minutes prior to grilling.
2. Ignite the charcoal, allowing the coals to turn white before placing the fish on the grill. Grill the swordfish steaks 3 to 5 minutes per side, depending on the thickness of the fish. The steaks are cooked when an inserted skewer comes out warm to the touch.
3. To serve, place a dab of Salsa Verde on each steak and pass the remaining sauce on the side.

It is important that the fish be fresh, not previously frozen, and bought during the high season—summer and fall—when it is most flavorful. Sure you can buy swordfish year 'round in this country. The question is "do you want to?" Although this recipe can be executed with a home broiler, nothing equals the flavor obtained from charcoal grilling.

SALSA VERDE

¼ cup finely chopped
Italian parsley
3 tablespoons capers, rinsed,
and finely chopped
6 anchovy fillets, finely
chopped and mashed

1 teaspoon minced garlic
1 teaspoon Dijon-style
mustard
1½ tablespoons fresh lemon
juice
1 cup olive oil
pinch of salt

1. Place the parsley, capers, anchovy fillets, and garlic in a small bowl. Whisk in the mustard and lemon juice.
2. Gradually beat in the olive oil, adding salt and additional lemon juice to taste if necessary.

ZUCCHINI TRIFOLATI
Sautéed Zucchini

8 small zucchini
1 large onion, very
   thinly sliced

2 tablespoons unsalted butter
2 tablespoons corn oil
   salt

1. Soak the zucchini in cold water for 20 minutes to remove sand or grit. Dry and slice as thinly as possible.
2. Sauté the onion in butter and oil until golden. Add the zucchini and sprinkle lightly with salt. Stir the vegetables, shaking the pan over medium heat for 2 minutes or until the zucchini becomes translucent.
3. Season to taste and serve at once.

What makes a good chef is the willingness to taste as you go along. I tell the kitchen help, "I want you to taste this dish until you feel like you never want to see it again." By the end of a busy evening, I feel as though someone has rubbed cotton batting across my palate. You still have a responsibility to the client to taste each dish before it goes out.

ZUCCOTTO
Tuscan Cake

6 *eggs, separated*
1 *cup plus 2 tablespoons*
  sugar
1 *tablespoon vanilla extract*
2 *cups less 2 tablespoons*
  sifted flour
2 *tablespoons cornstarch*
2 *cups whipping cream,*
  chilled

¾ *cup confectioners' sugar*
⅓ *cup blanched almonds,*
  toasted and chopped
3 *ounces chocolate chips,*
  chopped
¼ *cup unsweetened cocoa*
¼ *cup Cognac*
¼ *cup Cointreau*
¼ *cup maraschino liqueur*

1. Preheat oven to 350°.
2. Butter and flour a square 9-inch cake pan.
3. Beat the yolks, 1 cup sugar, and vanilla extract by hand or in a mixer until the mixture falls in a thick ribbon from the whisk or electric beater.
4. In a separate bowl, beat the egg whites to soft peaks and sprinkle in the remaining two tablespoons sugar. Continue beating until stiff.
5. Stir a quarter of the stiffly beaten egg whites into the yolk mixture to lighten it, then carefully fold in the remaining whites. Sift the flour and cornstarch over the egg mixture, then gently incorporate.
6. Pour the batter into the pan and bake in preheated oven for 40 minutes or until an inserted skewer comes out clean. Turn the sponge cake onto a cake rack and cool completely.
7. While the cake is cooling, whip the cream with the confectioners' sugar until very stiff. Divide the whipped cream into two bowls and fold the chopped almonds into one. In the other bowl, fold in the chocolate chips and cocoa.
8. Combine the liqueurs in a shallow dish. Cut the cooled sponge cake into slices ⅜-inch thick and soak the slices in the mixture of liqueurs for 10 minutes.
9. Line a perfectly round 1½-quart bowl with dampened cheesecloth, then follow with the cake slices; leave no gaps through which the filling can escape.

10. Spoon the cream/almond mixture into the cake-lined bowl, followed by the cream/chocolate mixture. Place the remaining cake slices on top and cover with waxed paper.

11. Freeze for at least 3 hours, but remove from freezer one-half hour before serving. Invert onto a round platter and serve at once.

This recipe has been graciously provided by our friend Anna Tomasi Nathanson, a first-rate Italian cook and teacher from Florence, Italy.

Dinner for Eight

Smoked Salmon Mousse

Scallop Soup with Vegetables

Veal Medallions with Stilton Sauce

Pineapple with Peppercorns, Caramel and Raspberry

Wines:

Chateau St Jean, Belle Terre Vineyard, Chardonnay, 1981

Jordan Vineyards Cabernet Sauvignon 1978

David Woodward, Chef

When Apley's opened at the Back Bay Sheraton in 1979, it revolutionized hotel dining in Boston. Gone forever were the days of stodgy Continental menus, of snooty maitre d's fussing with silver platters and tableside carving while your food froze. Apley's founding chef Robert Brody, and executive chef Jeffrey Worobel applied the innovations of French *nouvelle cuisine* to native foods of New England. Apley's current chef, English-born David Woodward, continues to make the starchless sauces and artful plate presentations of the "new" cooking today.

Given the proximity of the Sheraton world headquarters to the Sheraton-Boston hotel, it is not surprising that the corporation wanted to make Apley's its signature restaurant. The dining room received a million dollar facelift, transforming what was once an English-style pub into a sleek, split-level expanse of greys and silvers. Guests are seated on plush armchairs and sofas at tables set with Scandinavian glass and huge basket pattern service plates. The kitchen acquired a live trout tank and hydroponic herb garden, not to mention carte blanche to fly in fresh raspberries from New Zealand and fresh foie gras and truffles from France.

Named for a distinguished Bostonian of the turn of the century, Apley's was the first Boston restaurant to fill its water glasses with bubbly Saratoga Springs. Its open, glass wine "cellar," located at the rear of the dining room, specializes in California boutique wineries, as well as in classic French vintages. Unique to this stylish retaurant is "Apley's premier," a fixed price main course that enables guests to sample small portions of two different entrees on a single plate. Another elegant touch is the live harp or classical guitar music that graces the dining room nightly.

39 Dalton Street

SMOKED SALMON MOUSSE

oil
8 thin slices smoked salmon
6 ounces smoked salmon
3¼ cups heavy cream
   fresh white pepper and
      cayenne pepper to taste
3 ounces freshly grated
   horseradish

1 large cucumber, peeled,
   split, and seeded
juice of ½ lemon
salt and fresh black pepper
small jar black caviar
small jar red caviar

1. Lightly oil eight ½-cup glass or ceramic ramekins and line each with a slice of smoked salmon and chill.
2. Puree the remaining salmon in a food processor with ½ cup heavy cream and the peppers. Whip ¾ cup cream to stiff peaks in a chilled metal bowl, then gently fold in the salmon mixture.
3. Pack the mousse into the molds and fold the excess smoked salmon over the top. Chill the mousse in the refrigerator for at least 2 hours.
4. Prepare the sauce: place the horseradish, cucumber, 1½ cups cream, lemon juice, and salt and pepper in a blender and puree until smooth. Correct the seasoning to taste.
5. To serve, spread the sauce on eight chilled salad plates. Invert each ramekin to unmold the salmon mousse in the center of the plate on top the sauce. Garnish each mousse with a spoonful of red and black caviar.

Imagination is key to being a good chef. Here at Apley's we try to use local and seasonal ingredients. Our sauces are made without starchy thickeners.

SCALLOP SOUP WITH VEGETABLES

¾ cup Noilly Prat dry
   vermouth
1½ pounds bay scallops
3 small carrots, julienned
3 small or 2 medium leeks,
   julienned
1 bulb fennel, julienned

3 cups MUSSEL STOCK
3 cups FISH STOCK
   (see index)
1½ cups heavy cream
   salt and fresh white pepper
1 stick (4 ounces) unsalted
   butter

1. Heat the vermouth in a large saucepan and in it "sweat" the scallops (half-moon-shaped membrane from side of the shellfish removed) and vegetables; that is, cook them covered over a very low heat for 4-5 minutes. When the vegetables are soft (but still a little crisp) and the scallops translucent, transfer them to a soup tureen and keep warm.

2. Add the Mussel Stock and Fish Stock to the saucepan and simmer for 2 minutes. Add the cream and seasonings, bring the soup to a boil. Remove from the heat and whisk in the butter in small pieces. Pour this broth over the scallops and vegetables and serve at once.

MUSSEL STOCK

To make mussel stock, the next time you cook mussels, stem them in a large pot with a handful of chopped fresh parsley, a handful of finely chopped shallots, a bruised clove of garlic, a *bouquet garni* composed of bay leaf, thyme, black peppercorns, and a glass of white wine. Bring these ingredients to a boil, add the mussels, and cook, tightly covered, for 5 minutes or until the shells open. The steamed mussels are delicious eaten right out of the shells, and the liquid at the bottom of the pan is the mussel stock. Be sure to strain it, so as to avoid the sand at the bottom. Mussel stock can be frozen. Alternately, you can substitute bottled clam broth.

The vegetables are sweated in vermouth, not butter (as is usually the case), because the butter would leave a film on top of the soup.

VEAL MEDALLIONS WITH STILTON SAUCE

2 shallots, peeled and very
finely chopped
¾ cup dry white wine
2 cups heavy cream
4 ounces Stilton cheese,
(English blue)
fresh white pepper
2 red delicious apples
2 golden delicious apples

juice of ½ lemon
4 tablespoons butter
for sautéeing
8 (3 ounce) veal medallions,
cut from the loin
salt, fresh black pepper
½ cup CLARIFIED
BUTTER (see index)

1. Preheat oven to 350°.

2. Prepare the Stilton sauce: Combine the shallots and wine in a heavy, non-aluminum saucepan, and simmer until only a few spoonfuls of liquid remain. Add the cream, and stirring from time to time, simmer the sauce over a medium flame until its volume is reduced by half. Whisk in the Stilton in little pieces, then pour the sauce through a *chinoise* (China cap) or other fine meshed strainer. Correct the seasoning, and keep the sauce warm in a *bain marie* (pan of barely simmering water).

3. Prepare the garnish: Cut each apple into 8 wedges, and dip the wedges in a half and half mixture of water and lemon juice to prevent them from discoloring. Just before serving, sauté the apples to a light golden brown in butter.

4. Season the veal with salt and pepper. Heat the clarified butter in a sauté pan. Sauté the medallions over a medium-high heat for 2 minutes per side, then finish cooking in the oven for 3 minutes—the meat should remain slightly pink in the center.

5. Spoon the sauce onto the bottom two-thirds of each warm dinner plate, and place a veal medallion in the center of the sauce toward the dinner guest. Fan out the apple slices, alternating red and yellow, on the clean side of the plate over the veal for a garnish.

The best veal is called plume de veau *and it is available at any good butcher shop. Stilton is a famous blue cheese from England, and while Roquefort cheese would make an interesting sauce, there is really no substitute for Stilton.*

PINEAPPLE WITH PEPPERCORNS, CARAMEL AND RASPBERRY

1 ripe pineapple
  freshly ground black pepper
⅔ scant cup granulated sugar
¼ cup freshly squeezed
  orange juice
  juice of ½ lemon
6 tablespoons Crême de Cacao
6 tablespoons unsalted butter

2 cups RASPBERRY PUREE
2 pints vanilla or ginger
  ice cream
2 teaspoons canned green
  peppercorns
8 candied violets (available
  at gourmet shops)
16 fresh mint leaves

1. Trim off the skin of the pineapple and cut the fruit into ½ inch slices. Remove the core. Sprinkle the pineapple slices with black pepper.

2. Prepare the sauce: Place the sugar in a heavy, non-tin-lined saucepan over medium heat. Cook the sugar, stirring with a wooden spoon, until it melts and caramelizes (turns golden brown)—be extremely careful not to get any of the molten sugar on your hands.

3. Add the fruit juices (the mixture will hiss and sputter) and cook the mixture, stirring constantly, until the sugar is completely dissolved. Add 4 tablespoons Crême de Cacao and simmer for a few minutes. Remove from heat. Gradually whisk in 2 tablespoons butter.

4. Melt the remaining butter in a large frying pan and lightly sauté the pineapple slices over high heat. The fruit should be warmed through, and lightly browned at the edge. Add the remaining Crême de Cacao and flambé. Add the prepared sauce to the pan and bring to a simmer.

5. Meanwhile, spoon the Raspberry Puree in a circle on each of 8 dessert plates. Place a pineapple slice in the center. Top each slice of pineapple with a ball of ice cream and pour the hot sauce on top. Sprinkle the pineapple with a few green peppercorns and garnish each plate with candied violets and fresh mint leaves.

RASPBERRY PUREE

2   pounds fresh or frozen   ¼ cup confectioner's sugar,
        raspberries   or to taste
                                                    juice of ½ lemon, to taste

Puree the raspberries in a blender or food processor. (Do not over-puree, however, or you will crush the seeds and make the sauce bitter.) Force the puree through a fine mesh strainer and add sugar and lemon juice to taste.

This unusual dessert contrasts the sweetness of fresh pineapple with the exotic spiciness of black and green peppercorns. (Green peppercorns are the preserved fresh fruit of the pepper tree.) There are two ways to tell if a pineapple is ripe: the center leaves will pull out easily, and the base of the fruit should have a strong pineapple scent.

THE
Café Budapest

Dinner for Six

Chilled Tart Cherry Soup à la Budapest

Chicken Paprikas

Marinated Cucumber Salad

Fresh Raspberries with Grand Marnier Sauce

Wines:

With the Cherry Soup—Badacsony Szürkebarat

With the Chicken Paprikas—Tokaji Szamorodni

With the Dessert—Tokaji Aszu 5 Puttonyos

Edith Ban, Proprietor

Every evening at half past eight, a woman with regal bearing in a long white evening gown sweeps through the Café Budapest. As she pases, the maître d' snaps to attention, the waiters bustle more briskly and even the clients pause between bites, struck by an inexplicable but undeniable feeling of awe. The woman is Edith Ban, proud owner of the Café Budapest. There is no doubt in anyone's mind who is boss.

To look at Mrs. Ban today, one would never guess that she came to the United States as a refugee from the 1956 Hungarian Revolution and that during her first three months in Massachusetts she worked as a maid on Cape Cod. Unhappy working for others, she soon opened a small espresso bar next to Beth Israel Hospital in Brookline. By 1965, she had amassed the resources and cooking experience necessary to open a restaurant in the basement of the Lenox Hotel downtown. The Café Budapest started with four employees; today it has a staff of seventy. It is not uncommon for the Café Budapest to serve 500 dinners on a busy Saturday night.

"I still work in the kitchen," says the chic Mrs. Ban who prepares the restaurant's soups and sauces. She developed all the recipes used at the Café Budapest and the chefs are expected to follow these recipes to the letter. "The chefs may change, the food does not change at the Café Budapest," she insists. "We have no steam table or fryolator in the kitchen, so all of our central European fare is prepared to order."

The majesty and romance of the Austro-Hungarian empire still flourish at the Café Budapest. Guests are seated in three stately dining areas: the oak-paneled Hungarian Room, the elegant Pink Room and a charming, gingerbread-house-like Weinstube. In the Budapest bar, with its Empire fauteuils and flocked wallpaper, guest can sip heady Viennese coffee or golden Hungarian dessert wine and listen to the gypsy musicians who often fill the room with their haunting tunes.

90 Exeter Street
266-1979

CHILLED TART CHERRY SOUP Á LA BUDAPEST

2 (16-ounce) cans pitted
   tart cherries
1 large cinnamon stick
10 whole cloves
10 whole allspice berries
1 thin slice lemon

½ cup sugar
   pinch of salt
1½ teaspoons flour
1 cup medium cream
¾ cup dry Burgundy wine
½ cup heavy cream

1. Reserve the juice from one can of the cherries; drain the second can. Combine the cherries, the cherry juice from one can, the cinnamon stick, cloves, allpice, lemon, sugar, and salt in a saucepan and bring to a boil for 3 minutes.
2. Mix the flour with a few tablespoons medium cream to make a thick paste. Stir this paste into the remaining medium cream.
3. Add the cream and wine to the cherry mixture and boil for 1 minute. Remove the soup from the heat and let cool, then refrigerate.
4. To serve, ladle into soup bowls. Whip the heavy cream to stiff peaks and place a spoonful of the whipped cream on each serving. Store leftover soup in the refrigerator. It will keep for up to 2 weeks.

Note: In this recipe, medium cream refers to whipping cream that contains 30 to 36% butterfat. The heavy cream refers to whipping cream that contains 36 to 43% butterfat. Supermarkets customarily carry whipping cream with no indication of butterfat content and whether it is light, medium, or heavy. The enterprising gourmet must obtain the specified cream from a creamery or specialty food store.

This recipe calls for tart or sour cherries. You just won't get the same results if you use Bing cherries or substitute light cream for medium cream.

There is nothing difficult about these recipes. If you bring a little love to your cooking, you can prepare anything.

CHICKEN PAPRIKAS

2 *tomatoes*
1 *cup chicken fat*
2 *medium-size onions,*
   finely chopped
2 *cloves garlic, crushed*
2 *green peppers, cored,*
   seeded and thinly sliced
2 *(1½-pound) chickens,*
   each cut into 8 pieces
2 *tablespoons Hungarian*
   paprika

½ *teaspoon crushed hot*
   Italian red pepper
2 *cups chicken stock or 4*
   bouillon cubes dissolved
   in 2 cups hot water
   (approximately)
3 *tablespoons flour*
1 *pint sour cream*
1 *cup medium cream*
   salt and pepper
   NOCKERL

1. To peel the tomatoes, score an "x" on the bottoms, immerse in boiling water for 10 seconds, rinse under cold water and slip off skins. Remove seeds and coarsely chop. Set aside.

2. Melt the chicken fat in a heavy pan and sauté the onions over high heat until transparent and straw colored. Lower heat and add the garlic, green peppers, and tomatoes. Sauté until the peppers are softened and golden. Add the chicken pieces and lightly sauté—the meat should not be allowed to color.

3. Add the paprika, crushed red pepper, and enough chicken stock to cover. Gently simmer over low heat for approximately 20 minutes or until the chicken is cooked. (The juices will run clear when the meat is pricked with a fork.) Remove chicken from sauce and keep warm.

4. Whisk the flour into the sour cream and medium cream to make a cold roux. Whisk this roux into the sauce, bring the sauce to a boil and boil for 1 minute or until the sauce thickens.

5. Correct the seasoning. Strain the sauce onto the chicken and serve with Nockerl.

We only use butter and chicken fat in our cooking at the Café Budapest.

This recipe serves serves eight to ten.

NOCKERL

¼ cup butter, plus extra   1 teaspoon salt
     for tossing   2-2½ cups flour
6 whole eggs

1. Melt the ¼ cup butter and allow it to cool. Beat the eggs with the melted butter and salt.
2. Mix in the flour by hand to obtain a thick, stiff dough. Knead lightly and pat into a flat oblong.
3. Bring a large pot of salted water to a boil. Lay the dough on a small cutting board and cut off ⅛-inch strips of dough with the edge of a spatula directly into the boiling water.
4. Cook for 1 minute, then remove with a slotted spoon and drain. Toss with butter for serving.

Hungary is one of the oldest wine-producing countries in the world. The Romans imported Hungarian wine to Italy. Louis XVI preferred Hungarian Tokaji with fish. We serve only Hungarian wines at the Café Budapest and we have one of the most extensive selections in the country.

Paprika has been used in Hungary since the fifteenth century. We have the best paprika in the world because our climate is so well suited to its cultivation. People think Hungarian paprika is spicy. It is tasty and flavorful, but not spicy.

MARINATED CUCUMBER SALAD

1 cup white vinegar
½ cup sugar
2 cloves garlic, peeled
   and bruised
salt and freshly ground
   black pepper

3 large cucumbers, peeled
   and thinly sliced
1 small onion, thinly sliced
1 green pepper, cored, seeded
   and thinly sliced
½ cup sour cream

1. Combine the vinegar, sugar, garlic, salt and pepper for the marinade and marinate the cucumbers for as long or as little as you like. (You can serve them immediately or marinate them for up to 2 weeks.)
2. Serve the cucumbers with the onion and green pepper on chilled salad plates, with spoonfuls of sour cream on top.

There is nothing so perfect that it cannot be improved.

*In Hungary we have a problem of what to eat. In America they have a problem of what **not** to eat!*

I had never seen the inside of a restaurant kitchen before I opened the Budapest. If I had, I would surely have chosen another profession!

FRESH RASPBERRIES WITH GRAND MARNIER SAUCE

3 cups fresh raspberries
  dry red wine
5 egg yolks
½ cup plus 2 tablespoons
  sugar

½ cup Grand Marnier
1 cup heavy cream

1. Wash the raspberries in red wine, drain and set aside.
2. Beat the yolks with ½ cup sugar in a stainless steel bowl over a pot of hot water. Beat for 10 minutes or until the yolk mixture falls from the whisk in a thick ribbon. Remove from heat and stir in half the Grand Marnier. Let the sauce come to room temperature, then refrigerate until completely chilled.
3. Beat the cream with the remaining 2 tablespoons sugar to semi-stiff peaks. Gently fold the cream into the chilled yolk mixture with the remaining Grand Marnier.
4. Serve the raspberries in chilled champagne glasses, with the sauce spooned over the top.

When we put a dish on the menu, we always serve it at the price marked. If the cost of the ingredients has skyrocketed, that's too bad for us.

The Café Plaza

Dinner for Four

Oysters Kirkpatrick

Watercress Salad with Lemon-Walnut Dressing

Côtes de Boeuf Sauce Roquefort
(Prime Rib Steaks with Roquefort Sauce)

Roast Potatoes with Garlic

Strawberries Flambé

Wines:

With Oysters—Chardonnay, Freemark Abbey

With Meat—Gevrey–Chambertin Domaine Poulette,
Villamont

Christian Gallice, Chef

CAFÉ PLAZA

"A hotel isn't supposed to have such good food," a client once joked with the chef of the Cafe Plaza. "We run our restaurant as a restaurant, not a convenience eatery for hotel guests," was the quick, but convivial reply. The hotel is that grande dame of Boston hostelry, the Copley Plaza.

Built in 1912 as the sister hotel to New York's renowned Park Plaza Hotel, the Copley still retains the splendor of the turn of the century. Waterford crystal chandeliers cast a soft glow on the handsome oak *boiserie* of the Cafe Plaza dining room. Tuxedoed maître d's glide discreetly beneath one of Boston's most ornate stucco ceilings. With such luxurious appointments, one can easily see why the Cafe Plaza was named by United Airline's *Mainliner* magazine as one of the ten most romantic restaurants in the United States.

The Cafe Plaza, which has a newly instituted taster's menu, combines French classical with experimental cooking. A recent addition to the Best of Boston awards that the restaurant has garnered was for Best Breakfast. More affordable than dinner, the breakfasts here are a lofty way to start the day: goblets of freshly squeezed orange juice served on doillies, billowy pumpkin spice muffins with miniature jars of imported marmalade, and omelettes with apples and boursin. The Cafe Plaza wine list—stocked with the finest vintages of the last century—has received national attention.

Copley Plaza
267-5300 ext 1298

OYSTERS KIRKPATRICK

16 large fresh oysters in
    the shell
    MARINARA SAUCE
1 small green pepper, cored,
    seeded, and finely diced

1 cup grated sharp Cheddar
    cheese or Coon cheese
2 strips bacon, cut into
    16 (1") squares

1. Preheat oven to 450°.
2. Scrub the oysters thoroughly under running water and open them not more than 20 minutes before you plan to serve them.
3. Set oysters on the half shell on a baking sheet and spoon 1 teaspoon Marinara Sauce over each oyster. Place 1 teaspoon diced green peppers on top of the sauce. Sprinkle the oysters with the cheese and top with a square of bacon.
4. Just prior to serving, bake for 5 to 7 minutes or until the bacon starts to crisp around the edges. Serve immediately.

Note: Coon cheese is a sharp, tangy, crumbly cheese made from cow's milk that improves with age; it resembles sharp cheddar.

I have always liked the name of this dish. It's very Irish and very Boston.

The oysters you buy should be dirty. When oysters come out of the water, they live off the silt and grit on the shell. Clean oysters may look pretty, but they're actually starving to death

CAFÉ PLAZA

MARINARA SAUCE

3 cloves garlic, minced
¼ cup olive oil
1 small can Italian plum
  tomatoes, drained and
  chopped

pinch of oregano
¼ cup fresh chopped parsley
  salt and freshly ground
  black pepper

Sauté the garlic in the olive oil, but do not let brown. Add the tomatoes, oregano, parsley, salt and pepper and simmer for 10 minutes. Let the sauce cool before using it in the Oysters Kirkpatrick.

WATERCRESS SALAD WITH LEMON-WALNUT DRESSING

2 bunches watercress
½ clove garlic
salt
juice of 1-2 lemons

pinch of oregano
pepper
½ cup walnut oil
lemon wedges

1. Wash the watercress, shake to remove excess water and twist off the coarse stems. Place in a plastic bag in the refrigerator for 1 hour to crisp.
2. Mash the garlic with the salt. Combine with the lemon juice, oregano, and pepper in a salad bowl.
3. Whisk in the walnut oil little by little to obtain an emulsified dressing. Correct the seasoning, adding additional lemon juice if necessary.
4. Gently toss the watercress with the dressing. Serve on chilled salad plates with lemon wedges for garnish.

When choosing watercress, look for a bright emerald green color. Avoid bunches with yellow spots . . . People should avoid cutting the ends off lemon wedges or snapping off the pretty ends of string beans. I like my food to look the way it does in nature.

My advice to nonprofessionals is to not be afraid to undercook foods. Beef tastes best rare; fish is more delicate slightly undercooked; vegetables taste better left slightly al dente. The worst thing you can do to most food is to overcook it.

Use a recipe as a guideline, not a computer program. When I look at a recipe, I never read the amounts. I consider the ingredient combinations, then I let my imagination run free.

CÔTES DE BOEUF SAUCE ROQUEFORT

2 (3" thick) prime double-rib   salt and freshly ground
   steaks, with ribs   black pepper
   vegetable oil   SAUCE ROQUEFORT

1. Preheat oven to 400°.
2. Scrape the rib ends clean to French with decorative crowns.
3. Salt and pepper the steaks heavily and brown one side darkly in hot oil in a large skillet. Pour off fat, invert steaks in the skillet and roast in oven for about 20 minutes. (Rare beef will feel slightly springy when pressed with a finger.)
4. Remove the beef from the oven and let rest for 10 minutes.
5. To serve, carve each steak toward the bone into ¼-inch slices. Arrange these slices on hot dinner plates. Serve with Sauce Roquefort on the side.

You have to use genuine French Roquefort cheese for this dish. Blue cheese simply does not have the right flavor...The clue to good meat is the color, which indicates that the beef has been well aged. As soon as you get meat home from the market, remove the plastic wrapping; beef which sits in the package gets all wet and soggy. You want the meat to roast when you cook it, not steam.

CAFÉ PLAZA

SAUCE ROQUEFORT

4 ounces French Roquefort
  cheese
½ cup unsalted butter
1 bottle dry white wine

¾ cup whipping cream
salt and freshly ground
  black pepper

1. Mash the Roquefort cheese with the butter and beat with a wooden spoon or whisk until the mixture is smooth and creamy.
2. Pour the wine into a saucepan and boil until only ⅓ cup remains. Add the cream and reduce again by boiling until only ⅓ cup remains.
3. Reduce heat to low and whisk in the cheese/butter mixture, 2 tablespoons at a time. At no point should the sauce boil.
4. Strain the sauce and taste for seasoning; you will probably not need salt because the cheese is already salty. The sauce can be prepared ahead of time and kept at a blood-warm temperature over hot water.

ROAST POTATOES WITH GARLIC

4 Idaho or large Red Bliss
   potatoes, peeled and
   quartered
½ cup unsalted butter

10 cloves unpeeled garlic
   salt and freshly ground
   black pepper

1. Preheat oven to 400°.
2. Boil the potatoes in salted water for exactly 10 minutes, then drain. This can be done up to 24 hours ahead of time.
3. Place the potatoes in a roasting pan just large enough to accomodate them without crowding. Sprinkle liberally with salt and pepper. Add the unpeeled garlic cloves and dot the potatoes with the the butter.
4. Roast in oven for 30 minutes or until well browned, turning the potatoes once or twice to assure even roasting. Serve with or without garlic according to taste.

Note: The skin of the garlic must be completely intact, or the garlic will burn or go bitter. Do not use the cloves with skins which are split or cracked. The garlic can be discarded or eaten—the whole roast cloves look very pretty with the potatoes.

Correct seasoning is the cook's first duty. The diner should never need to pick up a salt or pepper shaker. When I'm served a dish in a restaurant, I assume the chef has seasoned the food as he meant for me to taste it. If there's not enough salt or pepper, that's too bad.

STRAWBERRIES FLAMBÉ

2   pints strawberries, washed
    hulled and halved
3   tablespoons sugar
    juice of ½ lemon

¼   cup strawberry-flavored
    brandy
2   tablespoons butter
    sprinkle of cinnamon
¼   cup Cognac

1. Place the strawberries in a shallow bowl with 2 tablespoons of the sugar, the lemon juice, and strawberry-flavored brandy. Let marinate for 10 minutes, turning once.
2. Heat a sauté pan over a chafing dish and add the remaining 1 tablespoon sugar and the butter, cooking until the mixture caramelizes. Quickly add the strawberries and marinade and sprinkle with cinnamon.
3. Pour the Cognac over the fruit and ignite. Remove the berries after 30 seconds—they should be barely warmed, not cooked—and finish flambéing the sauce. Serve the strawberries plain, on ice cream, or with whipped cream, spooning the sauce on top. Serve at once.

I never thought I would like Strawberries Flambé. I don't believe in cooking fruits like berries. But one evening, after a particularly grueling service, our maître d', Heinz Bunger, prepared this dish for me and it was wonderful!

Casa Romero

Dinner for Four

Sangrita

Caldo de Mejillones

Ensalada de Guacamole

Puerco Adobado

Arroz à la Mexicana

Flan al Coñac

Beer:

Light—Superior or Carta Blanca

Dark—Dos Equis

Leo Romero, Proprietor

"I started in the food business because there were no decent Mexican restaurants in New England," says Back Bay restaurateur Leo Romero. Armed with an innate ability to cook and the unshakable conviction that authentic Mexican fare could rival any cuisine in the world, Leo opened the Casa Romero on the ground floor of a Gloucester Street townhouse in 1972. "The menu was already printed and I had no idea how we were going to manage some of the dishes in a restaurant kitchen," he says, recalling the early days with a smile. Manage he did, though, and before long the Casa Romero was ranked the top Mexican restaurant outside of Mexico by *Gourmet Magazine* and one the ten best restaurants in the United States by the German guide book *Bessers*.

"Mexico has always had an exquisite cuisine," says Romero. "In Aztec times, fresh fish reached Mexico City more quickly by runner than it does by truck or locomotive today. When the Emperor Montezuma craved ice cream, he dispatched his cooks to fetch snow from the nearby mountains. Many modern Mexican specialties were invented during the Baroque period, when Mexico had one of the wealthiest aristocracies in the world."

The Mexican cuisine of the Casa Romero has little in common with the tacos and enchiladas of fast food chains, the mere thought of which makes Romero bristly. "Some of our sauces take three days to prepare, using dozens of ingredients, which must be specially and individually processed beforehand."

When it comes to Mexican cooking, Romero should know what he's talking about. The son of a Spanish-American diplomat and a Franco-Mexican mother, he grew up is Mexico, inhabiting all of the major provinces. "I have never set foot in a cooking school and I've trained some of the finest chefs in Boston," he says with pride. "I am a cook by avocation, by instinct, by love."

"When you open the door of the Casa Romero, you walk out of Back Bay and into Mexico," observes Romero. Colorful tile tables, straight-backed leather chairs, ornate wrought iron and Mexican handicrafts create the atmosphere of a Spanish colonial mansion. You also enter Leo Romero's home. "I consider the dining room downstairs an extension of my own dinner table," says Romero, who lives on the top two floors of the building. "I recieve my clients not so much as customers, but as guests."

30 Gloucester Street

SANGRITA

1 cup unsweetened grapefruit juice	1 tablespoon juice from canned jalapéno peppers
1 cup tomato juice	2 tablespoons grenadine

Combine ingredients and serve in cordial glasses.

Sangrita traditionally accompanies tequila and both are drunk before the meal, never at the table. In Mexico everyone has an individual version of Sangrita; this recipe comes from Casa Romero.

Mexican cooking is probably the most misunderstood cuisine in the world. If you study the history of Mexico, if you understand the geography and the people, it will become clear to you that the haute cuisine of Mexico is much more embellished, much more elaborate, much more lavish than the cuisines of France or the Austro-Hungarian Empire.

CALDO DE MEJILLONES
Steamed Mussels in Herbed Wine Broth

2 *pounds mussels*
1 *medium-size onion, very*
   finely chopped
½ *cup unsalted butter*

1 *cup finely chopped parsley*
   salt and freshly ground
   black pepper
1 *cup dry white wine*

1. Wash the mussels in several changes of cold water, thoroughly scrubbing the shells. Remove threads and discard any mussels with cracked shells or which fail to close when tapped.
2. Sauté the onion in the butter in a large saucepan until transparent. Add the parsley and a little salt and pepper. Pour in the wine and boil to reduce the mixture by half.
3. Place the mussels in the pan, cover, reduce heat, and steam for 5 minutes or until the shells open. Serve the mussels and broth in deep bowls with an extra bowl on the side to hold the empty shells.

We use aquacultured mussels, which contain virtually no sand or grit.

I don't approve of making a sacrament of fine food. Food should be enjoyed as a gustatory and biological necessity.

The best cooks in Mexico are illiterate for the most part. They are the maids, the peasant women, who have been cooking for generations and generations—almost forever.

ENSALADA DE GUACAMOLE

3 ripe avocados
1 cup CASERA SAUCE

4 large lettuce leaves
   fried tortilla chips

1. Peel the avocados and remove the seeds. Mash the flesh in a non-metallic bowl and gradually work in the Casera Sauce.
2. Mound the guacamole on lettuce leaves on four serving plates and serve with tortilla chips.

This guacamole is made with spicy Casera Sauce. Be sure to use very ripe California avocados. Floridu dues not grow avocados—they grow alligator pears and there is a difference.

There is no substitute for cilantro, the pungent leaves of the coriander plant. Cilantro can be found in most Hispanic, Chinese and natural food markets—it often goes by the name of Chinese parsley.

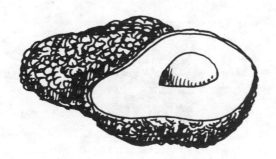

ARROZ A LA MEXICANA

2 cups unpolished long-
   grain rice
½ cup chicken fat or
   vegetable oil
½ cup CASERA SAUCE

4 cups homemade chicken
   stock
salt and freshly ground
   black pepper

1. Wash and rinse the rice in several changes of water to remove excess starch. Spread on a cookie sheet to dry.
2. Sauté the rice in fat in a large cast-iron frying pan until the grains are uniformly light brown.
3. Reduce heat to very low and stir in the remaining ingredients. Press a sheet of tin foil over the rice and cover with a heavy lid.
4. Cook over a low heat for 20 minutes. Do not uncover the pan or stir. Make sure the pan is correctly centered over the flame. When the rice is cooked, fluff with a fork and correct the seasoning before serving.

FLAN AL COÑAC

3 cups milk
4 eggs
1¾ cup sugar
⅔ teaspoon vanilla extract
⅓ teaspoon nutmeg

⅓ teaspoon cinnamon
⅓ teaspoon ground allspice
3 tablespoons Cognac
   pinch of salt

1. Preheat oven to 350°.
2. Scald the milk, but do not boil. Set aside to cool.
3. Beat the eggs well with ¼ cup of the sugar, vanilla, nutmeg, cinnamon, allspice, Cognac, and salt. Whisk in the cooled milk.
4. Place the remaining 1½ cups sugar with water to cover in a heavy, non-tin-lined saucepan. Cook over a high heat without stirring until the mixture attains a rich, golden caramel color.
5. Remove from heat and distribute the caramel evenly among four 6-ounce ramekins. Swirl the cups to coat the sides and bottom of each dish. Work carefully—molten caramel is extremely hot.
6. Once the caramel has cooled, ladle the custard mixture into the cups and place the cups in a shallow roasting pan with 1 inch of boiling water. Bake in preheated oven for 1 hour or until an inserted skewer comes out clean. Cool completely before serving. To unmold, invert the ramekins over deep dishes and shake until the flan slips free.

Unlike the Spanish version of this dessert favorite, the Mexican Flan is richly flavored with spices and brandy. It unmolds more easily if served the following day.

CASERA SAUCE

4 large ripe tomatoes
½ cup finely chopped onion
1 canned jalapéno pepper,
   finely chopped
¼ cup finely chopped cilantro

1 tablespoon olive oil
½ teaspoon crumbled oregano
   salt and freshly ground
   black pepper

1. Slice the stem ends off the tomatoes and grate the tomatoes into a shallow bowl. (Grating peels the tomato at the same time.)
2. Add the remaining ingredients and mix.

Note: This makes two cups sauce. Use the remaining cup for the rice.

I prefer the canned jalapénos over the fresh; the canned are actually a little tastier, because they are marinated in vinegar.

PUERCO ADOBADO
Pork Tenderloin Marinated with Oranges and Smoked Peppers

¼ cup oil
 juice of 1 lemon
½ cup orange juice
 concentrate
 grated rind of 1 orange

1 clove garlic, peeled
2 chipotle peppers
1 teaspoon salt
2 pounds pork tenderloin
1 orange, thinly sliced

1. To prepare the marinade, purée all the ingredients except the pork and orange slices in a blender.
2. Place the pork in a shallow dish and spread all surfaces with the orange mixture. Marinate the pork in the refrigerator for at least 3 hours, preferably overnight.
3. One hour before cooking, remove the pork from the refrigerator. Preheat the broiler.
4. Transfer the pork to a roasting pan and broil for 10 minutes. Turn the meat and broil for 5 more minutes or until the pork is thoroughly cooked. (The marinade "cooks" the meat, so the overall cooking time will be reduced.) Do not overcook or the meat will be dry.
5. Garnish the pork with the orange slices for serving.

In Mexico, the pork would be marinated in the juice of the naranja agria, *an orange with an intensely tart flavor. One can achieve the same effect in this country with canned orange juice concentrate. There is no substitute for the chipotle pepper, however, with its unique smoky flavor. It's available canned in many good gourmet shops.*

Although lard is the preferred fat of Mexico, we don't use it much any more, because it's not particularly healthy. Nutrition and health play an important part in what we eat. So we've replaced the lard in most dishes with a good polyunsaturated vegetable oil.

cybele

ON THE WATERFRONT

Dinner for Four

Seafood Fettuccine

Chicken Fiorentina

Butter-Glazed Broccoli

Cybele's Salad

Tartelettes aux Pommes Chaudes Cazalis

Wines:

*With the Fettuccine and Chicken—Orvieto Classico
(Le Veletti Estate) 1976*

*With the Tartelettes—Holle Johannisberg Riesling Spätlese
(Weingut Hof Sonneck)*

*Rebecca Caras, Proprietor
Patrick Parthonnaud, Chef*

Rebecca Caras started in the food business in 1975 cooking for friends out of her home. Today she rules a culinary empire which includes a catering enterprise, two gourmet carry-out shops and a pair of highly praised restaurants. "Cybele was the mythological daughter of Earth and Sky and to the ancient Greeks she symbolized plentitude and pleasure," says Caras. "We hope Cybele's holds the same meaning for our guests."

Caras describes Cybele's fare as "eclectic seasonal," uniting classical French cooking techniques with the bold flavors of the Mediterranean and the health consciousnesss of contemporary America. "We try to serve honest food, food which tastes similar to what a good cook would prepare at home," she says. Caras believes that the food and the people should be the main visual elements of any dining area. The exposed brick walls and ceiling beams, the stunning shades of grey, mauve and lavender of the three dining rooms provide a perfect foil for enjoying one's food and one's dinner companions at the new Cybele's.

"I have always been impassioned by food," says Caras. "It was how we expressed ourselves when we were growing up. My mother was a superb cook, who could take ingredients on any level and assemble them in a way which made sense. It's not an easy life," conceded Caras, who works seven days a week. "You have to commit yourself to a profession which involves a lot of compromise in the rest of your life. When you consider the hours, the working conditions, the heat, you understand why so many cooks are temperamental."

Cybele's chef, Patrick Parthonnaud, shares Caras' conviction that food should be honest. "What we do here," he says, "is not *nouvelle*, more modern—light, tasteful, real food which pleases the eye and the mouth." Parthonnaud, who began his career at 13 learning the art of "butchering with elegance" at a charcuterie in Paris, has worked all over the world including France, Switzerland, South Africa, Nairobi, and at top restaurants in San Francisco and New York. He came to America because he believes that we are on our way to becoming a great culinary nation and because he likes American products—especially Texas meats, California wines, and Wisconsin cheeses. "My cooking is a conciliation," says the chef, "between French roots and American products."

240 Commercial Street
523-1126

SEAFOOD FETTUCCINE

½ pound mussels
½ pound scallops
16 large shrimp
½ pound whitefish fillet
    (preferably sole, scrod,
    or haddock)
2 cups dry vermouth
1 tablespoon finely chopped
    shallots
2 tablespoons unsalted butter
5 scallions, finely chopped

1 clove garlic, mashed
4 cups whipping cream
1 pound good-quality dried
    fettuccine
1 cup freshly grated
    Parmesan cheese
¼ cup finely chopped fresh
    parsley
salt and freshly ground
    black pepper

1. Thoroughly scrub the mussels under running water and remove strings. Pull off the small, half-moon-shaped muscle from the scallops and cut the scallops into uniform pieces. Peel and devein the shrimp. Cut the fish fillets into 1½-inch by 2-inch slivers.
2. Bring the vermouth to a boil with the shallots. Add the mussels, cover tightly, and steam for 3 to 4 minutes or until the shells open. Remove the mussels and strain the broth through a cheesecloth or clean dish towel into a large saucepan.

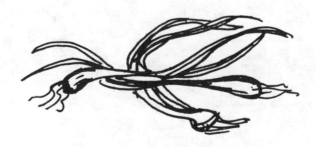

3. Reheat the broth and gently poach the scallops; they should be barely cooked. Remove the scallops with a slotted spoon and poach the shrimp until they begin to turn pink. Remove the shrimp and poach the fish. Each item will take 1 to 2 minutes to poach.

4. Melt the butter in a large sauté pan and sauté the scallions and garlic until soft and translucent. Add the fish-poaching liquid and the cream. Increase heat and boil the sauce until reduced by half.

5. Bring 6 quarts lightly salted water to a boil (a splash of oil helps prevent the fettuccine from sticking) and cook the fettucine al dente— about 8 minutes. Drain, but do not rinse.

6. To finish, add the pasta to the reduced sauce and simmer for 1 minute. Stir in the seafood, cheese, parsley, salt, and pepper. Simmer the mixture gently to warm the seafood.

7. Serve in bowls with a twist of freshly ground black pepper on top. Extra cheese should accompany the dish on the side.

The secret of cooking pasta is to watch it like crazy. We use Menucci pasta, which is the best dried pasta you can buy. We get the water really boiling, with a little oil to keep the noodles from sticking to one another. You have to stir constantly while the pasta is cooking.

To be a good chef, you have to be able to taste and to imagine taste. You have to be able to work with people, being both firm and supportive.

CHICKEN FIORENTINA

4 *plump artichokes*
1 *cup olive oil*
  juice of 3 lemons
¼ *teaspoon thyme*
  salt and freshly ground
    black pepper
½ *cup flour*

4 *boned chicken breasts,*
  trimmed, cut in half
  lengthwise, then in
  quarters against the grain
1 *cup vermouth*
¼ *cup finely chopped*
  fresh parsley

1. Cut the tops and stems off the artichokes. Remove the tough outer leaves and quarter. Use a spoon or paring knife to remove the fibrous "choke" from the center of each artichoke quarter.

2. Place the artichokes in a shallow pan with ½ inch olive oil, the juice of 2 lemons, the thyme, salt and pepper. Cover the pan and cook over low heat for 10 to 15 minutes or until the artichokes are tender. Remove the artichokes with a slotted spoon and set aside.

3. Lightly flour the chicken and gently sauté for 3 to 4 minutes in the artichoke oil without browning. Do not cook too long—if anything, the chicken should remain a little undercooked. Remove the chicken from the pan and set aside.

4. Pour off all but 2 tablespoons oil from the pan. Add the vermouth, remaining lemon juice, another pinch of thyme, salt, and pepper to the oil. Boil the sauce for 2 minutes. Return the chicken and artichokes to the pan to warm in the sauce. Stir in the parsley and serve at once.

The hardest thing about this dish is the sauce. You want to end up with an emulsion of olive oil, lemon juice and vermouth—a lovely, silky, translucent sauce, like a butter sauce—it's very tricky.

BUTTER-GLAZED BROCCOLI

1 *large bunch broccoli*
      (about 2 pounds)
¼ *cup unsalted butter*

1 *small red onion,*
      thinly sliced
   salt and freshly ground
      black pepper

1. Trim the tough stems from the broccoli and cut into florets.
2. Place the broccoli, 1 cup water, butter, salt and pepper in a saucepan and cook over high heat for 15 to 20 minutes or until most of the water evaporates and the broccoli is tender. When the broccoli is almost done, add the red onion slices. Serve at once.

You should always use unsalted butter. It's of a much higher quality. It's always fresher, because you can't disguise the rancidity with salt. Besides, you want to add the salt to suit your own taste.

CYBELE'S SALAD

1 large or 2 small heads
   Boston lettuce
8 cherry tomatoes, cut in half

¼ cup chopped scallions
1 cup RAC DRESSING

1. Wash and dry the lettuce, leaving the leaves whole.
2. Make four lettuce rosettes in the palm of your hand by laying successively small lettuce leaves on top of one another at right angles. If the lettuce has dark outside leaves, it's nice to alternate colors.
3. Garnish each lettuce rosette with cherry tomatoes and scallions. Spoon the RAC Dressing on top.

Cybele's Salad consists of lettuce leaves assembled to form a rosette. The RAC Dressing represents Rebecca A. Cara's initials.

RAC DRESSING

1 egg
2 tablespoons red wine
   vinegar
2½ tablespoons light cream
½ teaspoon lemon juice
½ teaspoon Dijon-style
   mustard

½ teaspoon sugar
1 clove garlic, minced
2 tablespoons olive oil
½ cup (scant) vegetable oil
   salt and pepper

1. Combine the egg, vinegar, cream, lemon juice, mustard, sugar, and garlic in a blender and mix.
2. Set the blender on low speed and gradually dribble in the oils. Season with salt and pepper before serving.

I don't like using food to intimidate people. You have to understand it, respect it, but you mustn't be afraid of it. Food is not a temple or a sacred involvement. Food is fun , it's humorous, it's an endless source of adventure.

TARTELETTES AUX POMMES CHAUDES CAZALIS

4 cup cold unsalted butter
2 cups flour
1¼ cups sugar
1 egg
  pinch of salt
2 Rome Beauty or McIntosh
  apples, peeled, cored,
  and cut in chunks
  juice of ½ lemon

zest of ½ lemon
1 teaspoon vanilla extract
4 firm apples (Granny Smiths
  or Golden Delicious),
  peeled and cored
  confectioners' sugar
1 cup softly whipped cream
1 cup sour cream

1. Pound the cold butter until it is softened. Sift the flour onto a counter top and make a well in the center. Break the butter into small pieces and place in the well along with ½ cup plus 2 tablespoons of the sugar, the egg, and salt.

2. Mix the ingredients in the center with your fingertips, gradually incorporating the flour to form large crumbs. Knead these into a compact mass with the heel of your palm. Chill the dough at least 20 minutes.

3. Preheat oven to 400°.

4. Roll the chilled dough on a lightly floured surface to a thickness of ⅛-inch. Line four 6-inch tartlet pans with the dough, pricking the bottoms with a fork to prevent the crusts from rising. Press a sheet of tin foil into each crust and fill the mold with dried beans or rice.

5. Refrigerate the tartlets for another ten minutes, then bake in preheated oven for 10 minutes. Remove the beans and tin foil and continue baking crusts 5 to 10 minutes longer or until completely cooked, but not browned. Carefully remove crusts from tartlet pans and leave to cool on a cake rack. Leave oven on at 400°.

6. Place the Rome Beauty or McIntosh apple chunks in a small saucepan. Add 2 tablespoons of the sugar, 1 tablespoon water, the lemon juice and zest, and vanilla extract. Cook over medium heat until the apples dissolve, forming a thick purée. Remove this compote from the heat and cool.

7. Using a sharp knife, cut a series of parallel, verical slashes ¼-inch apart on the four firm apples, turn the apples 90° and score in a similar fashion to achieve a crosshatch effect. Do not cut all the way through the apples—you want each piece of fruit to remain in one piece.

8. Sprinkle the apples with the remaining ½ cup sugar and bake in oven for 20 minutes or until the apples are browned and soft. The tartlets may be prepared ahead of time to this stage.

9. To assemble the tartlets, divide the compote evenly among the four tartlet shells. Using a spatula, carefully place the baked apples in the center. Just before serving, warm in the oven and sprinkle with confectioners' sugar.

10. Combine the whipped cream and sour cream to make an American approximation of crème fraîche. Serve on the side.

When you score the apples the first time, there is a very good chance they'll call apart. If this happens, you can piece them together with toothpicks.

These hot apple tartlets were the house dessert at the Henri IV, a two-star restaurant in Chartes. The owner of the restaurant, Maurice Cazalis, is a maître cuisinier of France.

Dinner for Four

Mushroom and Crab Strudel

Roast Cornish Game Hens with Lemon-Cumin Butter

Bibb Lettuce Salad with Pecan Vinaigrette

Almond Cream Peach Tart

Wines:

With the Strudel and Dessert—Joseph Perrier Champagne
Cuvée Royale 1973

With the Entrée—Spring Mountain (California)
Chardonnay 1977

Ben and Jane Thompson, Proprietors
Robert Kinkeade, Chef

Most people know Ben Thompson as the architect who redesigned the Faneuil Hall Marketplace. The same aesthetic excitement pervades Thompson's thriving Harvard Square eating establishment, the Harvest. Bright Marimekko fabrics (which Thompson introduced to the United States from Finland) and colorful food prints festoon the 180-seat restaurant/terrace café/nightspot. The entire dining room color scheme shifts twice yearly, green to brown to green, suggesting the eternal plantng and harvesting cycles.

But the visual is only part of the Harvest dining experience, and guests flock here for a cuisine that is as intriguing to the palate as the decor is exciting to the eye. Nouvelle cuisine is very much in vogue, and a spirit of innovation reigns. Chef Kinkeade orchestrates three different menus—lunch, dinner, and cafe—which change daily. Ris Lacoste's artful salads are evidence of a plentiful supply of fresh exotic ingredients.

"He encourages creativity," says Ris about the chef. Restaurant manager Stewart Jones adds that even though the employees are not actually related, "there is a feeling of family at the Harvest."

44 Brattle Street
Cambridge
492-1115

MUSHROOM AND CRAB STRUDEL

5 tablespoons butter
½ medium-size onion,
  chopped
¾ pound fresh mushrooms,
  washed and thinly sliced
5 ounces crab meat
3 tablespoons whipping cream

1 teaspoon arrowroot or
  cornstarch
2 tablespoons Madeira
  splash Worchestershire
  sauce
  salt and cayenne pepper
5 sheets filo dough
¼ cup dried bread crumbs

1. Preheat oven to 400°.
2. Melt 2 tablespoons butter in a shallow pan and sauté the onion until soft and transparant. Add the mushrooms and sauté for 5 minutes. Dice the crab meat into the pan and add the cream. Simmer for 1 minute.
3. Dissolve the arrowroot in the Madeira and stir it into the crab mixture. Simmer for 2 minutes, then season with Worcestershire sauce, salt and cayenne.
4. Melt the remaining butter. Carefully remove the filo dough from the package and stack on the work surface.
5. Brush the top sheet with melted butter and sprinkle with bread crumbs. Spread the mushroom-crab mixture along the bottom edge and roll around the stuffing to make a compact cylinder. Butter the second sheet of filo dough, sprinkle with more bread crumbs and roll around the crab cylinder. Repeat the process with the remaining filo, butter and bread crumbs.
6. Bake in oven for 18 minutes. Slice in fourths and serve.

Filo dough, sold in 1-pound packages of paper-thin sheets, is available in any Greek or Armenian grocery store and in the frozen gourmet food sections of many supermarkets as well.

When our chef tastes a dish, he knows exactly what it needs to bring out every subtlety. He's a fine-tuner.

ROAST CORNISH GAME HENS WITH LEMON-CUMIN BUTTER

4 *fresh Cornish game hens*
1 *pound unsalted butter,*
    at room temperature
1½ *tablespoons ground cumin*

juice of 1 large lemon
1 *teaspoon Worcestershire*
    sauce
pinch of salt and
    cayenne pepper

1. Preheat oven to 425°.
2. Rinse off the hens and pat dry.
3. Cream the butter and beat in the remaining ingredients.
4. To prepare the birds for stuffing, gently loosen the skin from the meat with your fingers. Spread the spiced butter under the skin, quite liberally around the breast area, reserving one-fourth for the outside of the bird. Truss the hens, sprinkle with salt and smear with the remaining butter.
5. Roast the birds in oven for 25 minutes or until the juices from the thigh run clear, basting often with the fat which accumulates in the roasting pan. Serve with rice pilaf or buttered noodles.

The secret to fine cuisine is good ingredients. I spend at least an hour a day on the telephone with my purveyors. I push them hard to supply me with what's freshest and best.

The first time I came to the Harvest, I saw the chef cooking a wild boar on the garden terrace. That alone convinced me I wanted to work here.

BIBB LETTUCE SALAD WITH PECAN VINAIGRETTE

1   head Bibb lettuce
    zest of ½ lemon
1   egg
1½ teaspoon Dijon-style
    mustard
1   cup vegetable oil
    juice of ½ lemon

    pinch fresh tarragon
    leaves
1½ tablespoons tarragon
    vinegar
1   tablespoon honey
½   cup finely chopped pecans
    salt and pepper

1. Separate and wash the lettuce leaves. Pat dry. Blanch the lemon zest in boiling water for 1 minute; rinse and drain. Set aside.
2. Whisk the egg with the mustard. Gradually whisk in the oil in a thin stream, followed by the lemon juice, blanched lemon zest, tarragon, vinegar, honey, pecans, salt, and pepper.
3. Toss the lettuce with the pecan vinaigrette and serve on chilled salad plates.

Note: The dressing can be whisked by hand or made in a blender or food processor. If using the latter, be careful not to overbeat.

ALMOND CREAM PEACH TART

2 cups plus 2 tablespoons all-purpose flour
1 teaspoon salt
¼ cup plus 1½ teaspoon sugar
¾ pound unsalted butter, at room temperature
4 egg yolks
3 tablespoons whipping cream

⅔ cup ground almonds
⅔ cup confections' sugar
1 egg
2 teaspoons Myers's rum
1 tablespoon cornstarch
½ cup milk
1 lemon peel
few drops vanilla extract
10-12 fresh peaches

1. To prepare the pâte royale, sift 2 cups flour onto a work surface and make a well in the center. Place the salt, 1½ teaspoons sugar, ½ pound butter, 2 egg yolks, and cream in the well.

2. Mix the liquid ingredients in the well with the fingertips, gradually incorporating the flour. Knead with the heel of the palm to obtain a smooth dough. Work the dough as little as possible. Chill the dough at least 30 minutes before rolling out.

3. Meanwhile, prepare the almond cream by creaming 6 tablespoons butter and beating in the almonds and confectioners' sugar. When the cream mixture is well blended, whisk in the egg. Beat in the rum and the cornstarch, whisking until themixture is light and smooth. Set aside.

4. To make the pastry cream, scald the milk with the lemon peel and vanilla extract. Whisk together the remaining 2 yolks, the remaining ¼ cup sugar, and the remaining 2 tablespoons flour. Pour the scalded milk into the yolk mixture, whisking constantly, and return the mixture to the saucepan. Boil vigorously for 3 minutes, stirring continuously to prevent scorching. Remove from heat, add the remaining butter, and leave to cool.

5. Preheat oven to 425°.

6. Remove the chilled pâte royale from the refrigerator and roll out to ⅛-inch thickness. Line a 9-inch flan ring or French tart pan with the pastry dough. Combine the almond cream with the cooled pastry cream and spoon the mixture into the pie shell.

7. Plunge the peaches into boiling water for 30 seconds; rinse under cold water. Remove the skins and slice each peach into 8 wedges. Arrange the peach slices on top of the filling in a decorative pattern.

8. Bake in oven for 25 to 30 minutes or until the almond filling is puffed and browned.

We make everything from scratch at the Harvest. All our sauces are made to order. All our vegetables are cooked to order. We have fresh produce delivery six days a week.

ICARUS

Dinner for Eight

*Sautéed Medallions of Sweetbreads with Tarragon and
Roasted Shallot Demi-Glace*

Chilled Melon Soup

Halibut Baked with Lobster Mousse and Pernod Sauce

Mango Lime Sherbet

Wines:

With the Appetizer—1981 Chateau "R"

With the Entree—1981 Stonegate Chardonnay

John Bellott and Tom Hall, Proprietors

Chris Douglass, Chef

ICARUS

The Icarus of Greek mythology was an overly curious lad, who strapped on wax wings and tried to fly to the sun. Boston's Icarus is a chic, but comfortable restaurant situated in a storefront in the historic South End. When Icarus first opened, nightly specials were informally scribbled on a blackboard. Guests now peruse a handsome, printed menu and formidable wine list, as this once casual neighborhood eatery has become a restaurant of citywide distinction.

Icarus owners John Bellott and Tom Hall expanded their restaurant recently, but both the old and new dining rooms retain the eclectic antique charm that makes Icarus so distinctive. Guests enter the restaurant through a stunning art nouveau stained glass portal, to be seated at mismatched Mission oak tables set with equally mismatched antique china and silver. The brick-walled dining area is filled with interesting artifacts, including a sculpture of Icarus posed for flight amid the indolently whirling ceiling fans.

Icarus chef Chris Douglass practices a highly personal version of *nouvelle cuisine*, improvising freely from French, Northern Italian, and even Oriental recipes. His eggs benedict and ham *pithivier* (puff pastry tart) have made Sunday brunch here a South End institution. His flourless chocolate gateau reduces even the most reserved dessert eaters to sighs.

540 Tremont Street

SAUTEED MEDALLIONS OF SWEETBREADS
WITH TARRAGON AND ROASTED SHALLOT DEMI-GLACE

1 pound fresh veal
   sweetbread
4 tablespoons CLARIFIED
   BUTTER (see index)
½ cup finely chopped carrot,
   onion, and celery mix
½ cup dry white wine
2 cups VEAL STOCK
   (see index)

6 shallots
2 tablespoons cognac
½ cup heavy cream
2 tablespoons chopped
   fresh tarragon
salt and fresh black pepper
flour for dusting
1 pound "angel's hair" lin-
   guine, or other fresh pasta

1. Soak the sweetbreads in cold water for 3-4 hours (or overnight), changing the water frequently. Drain and pat dry.

2. Heat 2 tablespoons butter in a skillet over a medium heat and sauté the vegetables for 3-4 minutes, or until they are soft and beginning to brown. Increase the heat to high and "deglaze" the pan with wine, that is, add the wine and scrape the skillet with a spatula to loosen any congealed pan juices. Boil the wine until only a few table-spoons are left.

3. Reduce the heat to medium, add the sweetbreads, and cook for 5 minutes, turning frequently and basting with vegetable mixture, or until the sweetbreads become firm and white. Season them lightly with salt and pepper, and add stock to barely cover. Adjust the heat so that the stock barely simmers, then cover the pan and braise the sweetbreads for 20 minutes, or until they are firm to the touch.

4. Remove the sweetbreads from the braising liquid, reserving the lat-ter for the sauce. Wrap the sweetbreads in cheese cloth or in a clean dish towel, and cool between two dinner plates weighted with a large can (or 5 pound bag of sugar). Note: weighting compresses and shapes the sweetbreads for ease in slicing and sautéeing them later. Prepare the sauce while the sweetbreads are cooling.

5. Preheat oven to 425°.

6. Boil the braising liquid, skimming off all of the fat that rises to the surface, until only 1 cup remains. Meanwhile, roast the shallots in buttered aluminum foil in the oven for 10 minutes. Slip off the shallot skins and coarsely chop them, then add to the reduced braising liquid and simmer for 10 minutes.

7. Puree the sauce and vegetables in a food mill or through a strainer (pressing with the back of a ladle). Place the sauce over medium heat and add the cognac and cream. Bring the sauce to a boil, add tarragon and salt and pepper to taste, remove from heat, and reserve.

8. To serve, unwrap the cooled sweetbreads, and slice them diagonally into ¼-inch thick medallions. Dust the medallions with flour, and sauté in the remaining 2 tablespoons butter until lightly browned on both sides.

9. Meanwhile, cook the pasta *al dente* in rapidly boiling, salted water. Drain it and divide neatly among eight warm appetizer plates. Arrange 2-3 sweetbread medallions on top of each mound of pasta and spoon the sauce over.

CHILLED MELON SOUP

1 medium-size ripe
   cantaloupe
1 medium-size ripe
   honeydew melon
1 cup fresh orange juice
   juice of 1 lemon
   juice of 1 lime
2 tablespoons honey

1 spice bundle (2 cloves, 2
   allspice berries, and 1
   stick cinnamon tied in
   cheesecloth)
1 cup light cream
1 cup sour cream, yogurt,
   or crème fraîche
   (see index) for garnish

1. Peel and seed the melons and cut into large cubes. Combine the melon, fruit juices, honey, and spices in a heavy saucepan and simmer gently over medium heat for 10-15 minutes, or until the melon is very soft. Discard the spice bundle, and puree the soup in a blender or food processor until smooth. Pour the soup into a large bowl and chill.

2. Just before serving, whisk in the cream. Ladle the soup into chilled bowls and garnish each with a dollop of sour cream.

This chilled melon soup will refresh the palate after the richness of the sweetbreads. It is important to use fresh fruit juice and melons that are as ripe as possible. The best way to tell if a melon is ripe is to smell the stem end. It should smell like ripe fruit.

HALIBUT BAKED WITH LOBSTER MOUSSE
AND PERNOD SAUCE

1 onion, sliced
2 carrots, peeled and chopped
1 rib celery, chopped
¼ cup fresh chopped parsley
1 clove garlic, peeled
3 ripe tomatoes, peeled
   and seeded
3 cups dry white wine
1 quart water
1 bay leaf
10 black peppercorns
1 (1¼ pound) lobster,
   female, if possible
4 pounds halibut
1 whole egg

salt, fresh white pepper
freshly grated nutmeg
3½ cups heavy cream
3 egg whites
   butter for the baking dish
1 tablespoon butter
4 shallots, finely chopped
¼ cup Pernod liqueur
2 tablespoons fresh chopped
   chervil
1 medium-size zucchini,
   core removed, and
   skin julienned
1 leek, julienned
1 carrot, julienned

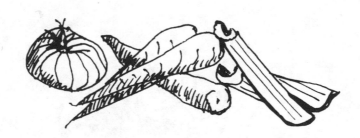

1. Prepare the lobster "essence": Place the onion, carrots, celery, parsley, garlic, tomatoes, wine, water, bay leaf and peppercorns in a large, enameled or stainless steel pot and boil for 5 minutes. Add the lobster and cool. Reserve the broth.

2. When the lobster is cool enough to handle, remove the meat and reserve. (The meat should be slightly undercooked—it will be used for making the mousse.) Reserve the tomalley and any roe (the former is green, the latter will be black because it is undercooked). Be sure to collect any juices. Discard the grey gravel sack in the head of the lobster and return the shells to the broth. Simmer for 30 minutes, strain the broth, and return it to a heavy saucepan. Boil the broth, stirring from time to time to avoid scorching, until only 1 cup liquid remains. This is the "essence" that will be used as a base for the sauce.

3. Prepare the lobster mousse: Remove the skin from the halibut and cut off an 8-ounce piece from the tail (this will be used for the mousse). Cut the remaining fish into 8 equal portions.

4. Puree the 8-ounce tail piece in the food processor along with the reserved lobster meat and the whole egg. Add the seasonings with the machine running, followed by 1 cup cream. This step can be done ahead of time, as the mousse needs to be refrigerated at least 30 minutes.

5. Just prior to baking, stir ½ cup cream into the mousse mixture with a spatula. Stiffly beat the egg whites with a pinch of salt. Gently stir a little of the egg whites into the mousse to lighten it, then gently fold this mixture into the remaining whites.

6. Preheat oven to 450°.

7. Generously butter a large baking dish and add the fish, skin side down, so that none of the pieces are touching. Spread one-eighth of the mousse mixture over each piece, covering the whole area. Bake the fish for 10-12 minutes, or until the mousse begins to brown and the fish becomes firm. The sauce can be prepared while the fish is baking.

8. To prepare the sauce, melt the butter in a stainless steel or enameled saucepan and add the shallots. Gently cook over low heat for 3 minutes, or until the shallots are soft and translucent. Add the Lobster Essence, increase heat to medium, and cook until only 4 tablespoons liquid remain.

3. Prepare the *americaine* sauce: Traditionally, this sauce is made with live lobster. To kill the lobster humanely, place it belly side down on a large cutting board. Holding the tail down with a dish towel, plunge a knife through the head directly between the eyes, and cut the lobster in half lengthwise. (This kills the lobster instantly, although the body may continue to wriggle.) Cut body and claws into 2-inch pieces, and reserve the lobster and juices in a bowl. Do this for two lobsters.

4. Melt 3 tablespoons butter in a large saucepan, and sauté the vegetables over high heat for 3 minutes. Add the lobster pieces and continue sautéeing for 2 minutes. Add the cognac and flambé. Add the white wine and boil until reduced by half. Add the tarragon, tomato paste and water, and simmer for 1 hour. Add the cream and cook the sauce for 15 more minutes. Strain the sauce through a "China cap" or other fine-meshed strainer, pressing hard with the back of a ladle, to extract the sauce from the shells. Correct the seasoning and reserve.

5. Boil or steam the remaining six lobsters for 6-8 minutes, or until cooked. Remove the fan section of the tail of each lobster, wash it off, and reserve for garnish. Cut each lobster in half lengthwise and remove the meat, reserving the prettiest half of the head section for garnish. Remove the meat, from the claws, and coarsely dice all the lobster meat. Keep it warm.

6. Meanwhile, prepare the vegetable garnish. Cook the green beans and asparagus separately in salted, rapidly boiling water for 3 minutes, or until crispy tender. Refresh under cold water (this fixes the bright green color and prevents overcooking). Note: the vegetables can be prepared ahead of time to this stage. Just before serving, melt 2 tablespoons butter in a frying pan and warm the vegetables in it. Melt the remaining 2 tablespoons butter in a smaller frying pan, and sauté the tomato over medium heat for 2 minutes, or until it begins to soften. Warm the ravioli, the sauce and the plates.

MANGO LIME SHERBET

2 pounds fresh, ripe mango	3 tablespoons fresh lime,
1½ cups water	or to taste
1 cup sugar	fresh mint leaves
	for garnish

1. Peel and dice the mango, reserving the pits. You should wind up with 3 cups fruit.
2. Combine the water and sugar in a heavy saucepan over moderate heat, stirring until the sugar is completely dissolved. Add the reserved mango pits, cover the pan, and simmer for 5 minutes.
3. Remove the pits and discard, scraping off and reserving any additional flesh. Pour the sugar mixture into a stainless steel bowl over crushed ice and chill for 1 hour.
4. Puree the diced mango with the sugar mixture in a blender or food processor, adding lime juice to taste. Chill for 2 hours.
5. Freeze the mango puree in an ice cream machine, following the manufacturer's directions. To serve, spoon the sherbet into frosted wine glasses and garnish with a sprig of fresh mint.

This dessert should be served as soon as possible after it is made. If too frozen, it becomes unpalatable, so remove it from the freezer to soften when you serve the entree.

This sherbet can also be made in the freezer section of the refrigerator. Place the mixture in a bowl in the freezer until almost frozen. Beat vigorously with a whisk, and return to the freezer. Continue freezing and beating the mixture 3-4 times, or until the desired consistency is achieved.

J·u·l·i·e·n

Restaurant Bar

Dinner for Six

Terrine de Celeri

Raviolis de Homard aux Truffes et Tomates Fraiches

Mille Feuilles du Julien aux Framboises

Wine:

Chablis 1er Cru "Les Vaillons" Defaix 1981

Bâtard Montrachet Delagrange-Bachelet 1979

Chateau Roumieu LaCoste 1979

Meridien Hotels (a subsidiary of Air France)

Michel Pepin, Executive Chef

Manicured espalier faces the limestone walls of the dining room. Black tied captains bustle amid stately Queen Anne wing-back chairs and tables set with heavy silver, soft lamplight, and fresh Peruvian lilies. Welcome to the restaurant Julien at the Hotel Meridien, where hotel dining is raised to a three-star art.

Owned and operated by Air France, the Hotel Meridien opened on August 24, 1981, in the old Federal Reserve building. Built in 1922, and modeled on a 16th century Roman palace, this historic landmark is one of Boston's finest examples of Renaissance Revival Architecture. The Julien, the hotel's formal dining room, occupies the former Members Court, and is decorated with custom carpets and ornately guilded ceilings. The Julien Lounge boasts paintings by N.C.Wyeth, not to mention nightly live piano music that spills over into the dining room.

The Julien is named for one Jean-Baptiste Julien, a French emigré who opened Boston's first French restaurant in 1793. There's nothing old-fashioned about the Julien's menu, however, which proposes the latest innovations of *nouvelle cuisine*. The Julien menu was originally designed by Gerard Vie, owner of the prestigious Les Trois Marches restaurant in Versailles. Michel Pepin, the restaurant's Beaujolais-born executive chef, remains commited to serving an inventive contemporary cuisine based on the principles of classical French cooking.

The formal Julien dining room is not the only restaurant at the Hotel Meridien. The stylish Cafe Fleurie draws an enthusiastic crowd for supper, dancing, and a lavish Sunday brunch.

250 Franklin Street
451-1900

TERRINE DE CELERI
Terrine of Celery and Duck Liver

1 medium-sized celeriac
1 pound duck livers, trimmed
3 sticks (¾ pound) unsalted
   CLARIFIED BUTTER
   butter for greasing the
   terrine mold

salt and fresh black pepper
1 head Boston lettuce,
   washed and dried
½ cup vegetable oil
1 stalk celery
12 cherry tomatoes

1. Preheat oven to 350°.
2. Peel the celeriac and place in a large saucepan in cold salted water to cover. Bring the water to a boil, and cook for 10 minutes, or until it is easily pierced with a paring knife. Immerse it in cold running water until cool. Cut the celeriac into slices ½ inch thick. Blot dry on paper towels and reserve.
3. Puree the duck liver in a blender or food processor. Slowly whisk in Clarified Butter, salt and fresh black pepper to taste. Force the mixture through a *chinoise* or fine meshed strainer. Brush a 1-quart terrine mold with the remaining melted butter.
4. Line the bottom of the mold with celeriac slices, add ½ inch of liver mixture. Repeat until all the ingredients are used up. Gently tap the pan to knock out any bubbles. Cover the terrine with a sheet of buttered aluminum foil. Set the mold in a roasting pan with ½ inch boiling water (this is called a *buin marie,* or "water bath," and it assures a moist, even heat for baking the terrine). Bake the terrine for 1 hour, or until an inserted skewer comes out clean.
5. Let the terrine cool to room temperature, then place a block of wood or a light weight on top to compact the terrine and chill overnight.
6. The next day, place the lettuce in a blender with the oil, salt and pepper, and puree to a light mousse. Correct the seasoning.
7. Peel the celery stalk with a vegetable peeler, and julienne it into 2 inch matchsticks.

8. To serve, carefully unmold the terrine (it may be necessary to dip the pan in hot water for a few seconds), and cut it into twelve slices. (It helps to heat the knife in hot water before slicing.) Spoon the sauce onto each plate, forming a circle, and arrange two slices of terrine on top. Garnish each plate with a pile of julienned celery and a cherry tomato.

Celeriac is the root of the celery plant. It is available a most large supermarkets and gourmet produce shops.

CLARIFIED BUTTER

To clarify butter, melt unsalted butter in a saucepan, and continually skim off the white skin that forms on the top with a spoon until none remains. Spoon the butter itself into a measuring cup, leaving behind the milky water at the bottom of the pan. When properly clarified, butter will keep almost indefinitely. Because clarified butter does not burn, it is ideal for sautéing and pan frying.

"I am continually amazed how eager my American chefs are to learn about cooking. Good food is a new-found fascination for the U.S.—in France we have been surrounded by it for centuries."- Michel Pepin

RAVIOLIS DE HOMARD AUX TRUFFES ET TOMATES FRAICHES
Lobster Ravioli with Tomatoes and Truffles

2 (1¼ pound) lobsters, cooked
½ cup heavy cream
Salt and fresh white pepper
1 pound (3 feet) fresh fettuccini sheets
Egg glaze (beat 1 egg with a pinch of salt)
2 quarts FISH STOCK (see index) or clam broth
8 live chicken lobsters
7 tablespoons butter
2 medium-size onions, finely chopped
2 carrots, peeled

3 stalks celery, finely chopped
11 ripe tomatoes, peeled and seeded
¼ cup cognac
½ cup dry white wine
1 tablespoon fresh tarragon leaves
2 tablespoons fresh tomato paste
1 quart water
½ cup cream
½ pound haricots verts (French green beans)
1 pound asparagus, ends snapped, peeled
1 small truffle, julienned

1. Puree the cooked lobster meat to a smooth paste in a food processor with the cream and seasonings. Load the mixture into a piping bag fitted with a ¼-inch round tip. Spread a sheet of pasta on a work surface, and pipe neat rows of hazelnut-sized mounds of lobster mixture on the pasta, leaving 2 inches between each mound and 1 inch to the edge of the sheet of pasta. Using a pastry brush, paint the pasta with egg glaze between each mound of lobster mousse. Place a second sheet of pasta on top of the first, pressing gently with your fingers around each mound to squeeze out any air bubbles. Using a fluted pastry wheel, cut between each mound to form 2-inch square ravioli. Repeat the procedure above until all the lobster mousse is used up: you should wind up with 25-30 ravioli.

2. To cook the ravioli, bring the fish stock to a boil, add the ravioli, and cook for 3-4 minutes, or until *al dente*. Drain and reserve in a warm place while you prepare the sauce.

3. Prepare the *americaine* sauce: Traditionally, this sauce is made with live lobster. To kill the lobster humanely, place it belly side down on a large cutting board. Holding the tail down with a dish towel, plunge a knife through the head directly between the eyes, and cut the lobster in half lengthwise. (This kills the lobster instantly, although the body may continue to wriggle.) Cut body and claws into 2-inch pieces, and reserve the lobster and juices in a bowl. Do this for two lobsters.

4. Melt 3 tablespoons butter in a large saucepan, and sauté the vegetables over high heat for 3 minutes. Add the lobster pieces and continue sautéeing for 2 minutes. Add the cognac and flambé. Add the white wine and boil until reduced by half. Add the tarragon, tomato paste and water, and simmer for 1 hour. Add the cream and cook the sauce for 15 more minutes. Strain the sauce through a "China cap" or other fine-meshed strainer, pressing hard with the back of a ladle, to extract the sauce from the shells. Correct the seasoning and reserve.

5. Boil or steam the remaining six lobsters for 6-8 minutes, or until cooked. Remove the fan section of the tail of each lobster, wash it off, and reserve for garnish. Cut each lobster in half lengthwise and remove the meat, reserving the prettiest half of the head section for garnish. Remove the meat, from the claws, and coarsely dice all the lobster meat. Keep it warm.

6. Meanwhile, prepare the vegetable garnish. Cook the green beans and asparagus separately in salted, rapidly boiling water for 3 minutes, or until crispy tender. Refresh under cold water (this fixes the bright green color and prevents overcooking). Note: the vegetables can be prepared ahead of time to this stage. Just before serving, melt 2 tablespoons butter in a frying pan and warm the vegetables in it. Melt the remaining 2 tablespoons butter in a smaller frying pan, and sauté the tomato over medium heat for 2 minutes, or until it begins to soften. Warm the ravioli, the sauce and the plates.

7. To assemble the dish, spoon the *americane* sauce in a circle on each plate. Arrange a neat row of lobster ravioli down the center. Pile the diced lobster meat on top of the ravioli. Place the reserved head and tail shells at either end of the ravioli and arrange the green beans and asparagus in an alternating fashion to resemble the legs of the lobster. Sprinkle the tomato and truffles on top. As the assembly of each plate is somewhat time consuming, it is best to place the finished plates in a warm oven briefly before serving.

To peel and seed tomatoes: Using a paring knife, cut the stem end out of each tomato and score an "X" on the bottom of each. Plunge the tomatoes in rapidly boiling water for 15 seconds, then run under cold water. The skin should pull off with your fingers. To seed the tomato, cut in half widthwise and ring the pulp and seeds out by squeezing with the palm of your hand.

"A good chef cannot be afraid of long hours. I typically work 14-15 hours a day. Sometimes I will go 3 months without a day off." - Michel Pepin.

MILLE FEUILLES DE JULIEN AUX FRAMBOISES
Almond Napoleans "Julien" with Raspberries

4 *ounces slivered almonds*
1 *cup sugar (save 2*
   tablespoons out)
2 *tablespoons flour*
3 *egg whites*
4 *egg yolks*
   a few drops pure vanilla
   extract

2 *tablespoons unsalted butter,*
   room temperature
3 *pints fresh raspberries*
   sugar and lemon juice
   to taste
2 *tablespoons confectioner's*
   sugar
1 *cup heavy cream, whipped*
   to stiff peaks

1. Preheat oven to 450°.
2. Combine the almonds, sugar, flour, egg whites, egg yolks, and vanilla in a blender or food processor, and puree until smooth. Thickly butter 2-3 baking sheets. Place spoonfuls of batter in neat rows on the baking sheets, leaving 6 inches between each and 3 inches to the edge of the baking sheet. Using a spatula, spread the batter in a circular manner to form a 3 inch circle. Bake the tiles for 3 minutes, or until golden brown at the edges. Using a metal spatula, gently slide the tiles off the baking sheet onto a cake rack and let cool.
3. Meanwhile, prepare the raspberry *coulis*. Puree 1 pint of the raspberries in a blender or food processor, adding sugar or lemon juice to taste. Force the puree through a fine meshed strainer to remove the seeds. Preheat the broiler. Mix the confectioner's sugar with the remaining 2 tablespoons of granulated sugar and sprinkle six of the tile cookies with it. Run them briefly under the broiler to caramelize the sugar. (Warning: molten sugar gives one of the worst burns in the kitchen. Be careful not to drip any on your fingers.)

4. To assemble the *mille feuilles*, spoon the raspberry *coulis* in a circle onto each of six chilled plates. Place an almond tile directly on top. Load the whipped cream into a piping bag fitted with a ¼-inch star tip and pipe a spiral of whipped cream onto each tile cookie. Arrange a layer of raspberries on top of the cream. Place the second cookie on top of the raspberries, and garnish with the remaining whipped cream and raspberries. Place the caramelized tile cookies on top and serve at once. Note: the individual component for the tile cookies can be prepared ahead of time, but be sure to store the *tuiles* in an airtight tin. Because of the delicacy of the cookies themselves, however, the *mille feuilles* must be served as soon as they are assembled.

LE BOCAGE

Dinner for Six

Shrimp and Cape Scallops Rémoulade

Fennel Soup

Rack of Lamb with Poivrade Sauce

Gratin Dauphinoise

Pineapple with Rum

Wines:

With the First Course and Soup—Champagne Brut

With the Lamb—Château Talot 1967

After Dinner—Sandeman Port 1963

Enso Danesi, Proprietor

LE BOCAGE

"You can't learn the restaurant business in five years," says Enzo Danesi. As owner and kitchen director of the eminently successful Bocage restaurant in Watertown, he should know. Born near Milano, Italy, Enzo began his career forty years ago. He worked in France, Germany, Switzerland and Greece before coming to Boston. After being told by his doctor to "take it easy" eight years ago, Enzo sold a booming eating establishment downtown to purchase a tiny Cambridge restaurant called Le Bocage.

"I always wanted a small place where I could do things right," muses Enzo. Within no time, crowds thronged to the Huron Avenue storefront. The success strained the tiny Bocage kitchen, forcing Enzo to move the restaurant to the more spacious site in Watertown that it occupies today.

Part of what makes Enzo's restaurant so popular is the "Bocage system," emulated by countless other eating establishments in the area. The Bocage's limited menu changes daily, assuring guests the freshest possible comestibles. The white walls and simple but tasteful décor—modeled after the country inns of Northern Italy—offer patrons comfortable dining without distraction. "My service is down to earth," says Enzo who prefers college students to professional waiters. "They say 'good evening' and everyone feels at ease."

72 Bigelow Avenue
Watertown
923-1210

SHRIMP AND CAPE SCALLOPS RÉMOULADE

24 large shrimp, peeled
  and deveined
COURT BOUILLON
1 pound Cape scallops
  lettuce leaves

RÉMOULADE SAUCE
3 tablespoons finely
  chopped parsley
2 tablespoons whole capers

1. Place the shrimp in cool Court Bouillon and heat slowly to poach the shrimp. Do not boil. The shrimp will feel firm to the touch when cooked, but taste one to make sure. Remove with a slotted spoon and chill.
2. Cool the Court Bouillon. When cool, add the scallops (with half-moon-shaped muscle on the side of the scallops removed) and re-heat slowly to gently poach until cooked. They should, of anything, remain a little under done. Drain scallops and transfer to a cool place to chill.
3. Line six small plates with lettuce leaves. Toss the seafood with the Rémoulade Sauce and mound in the center of the plates.
4. Sprinkle with parsley and capers before serving.

COURT BOUILLON

2 quarts cold water
2 tablespoons salt
1 onion, peeled and sliced
1 carrot, thinly sliced

Bouquet garni of bay leaf,
  thyme and parsley
10 whole peppercorns

Combine all ingredients in a large saucepan and simmer for 15 minutes. Strain and cool.

RÉMOULADE SAUCE

2 egg yolks
1 tablespoon Dijon-style
  mustard
  Dash vinegar
½ teaspoon salt
1⅓ cups vegetable oil
2 tablespoons olive oil
2 tablespoons red wine
  vinegar
1 small clove garlic, minced

1 anchovy fillet, finely
  chopped
1 tablespoon minced onion
2 tablespoons capers,
  rinsed and finely chopped
2 tablespoons finely
  chopped parsley
  salt and freshly ground
  black pepper

1. Whisk the egg yolks, mustard, dash of vinegar and salt in a heavy bowl or blender.
2. Gradually dribble in the oils, whisking continually, to make an emulsified mayonnaise.
3. Whisk in red wine vinegar, garlic, anchovy, onion, capers and parsley and season to taste.

We often run out of fish because I just buy the limit. I don't want anything to be left over for the next day.

Our favorite olive oil is made by the Berio Co., for vinegar we use Dessaux et Fils.

Most of the time I cook by look, smell and taste. Beware of pseudo-precision in recipes; it only gives you false confidence.

FENNEL SOUP

2 large leeks, trimmed,
  washed and sliced
2 bulbs fennel, thinly sliced,
  stalks and green leaves
  removed

1 small can imported
  Italian tomatoes
1 quart chicken stock
2 cups heavy cream
  salt and pepper

1. Place leeks, fennel, tomatoes and stock in a large pot and simmer for 1½ to 2 hours or until the vegetables are very tender.
2. Purée the soup in a blender and force through a fine sieve to remove vegetable threads and fibers. (A food processor does a very poor job on soups.)
3. Add the cream and salt and pepper to taste. The soup should have a distinct fennel flavor—if necessary, add a couple of splashes of Pernod.

I could not have opened a restaurant like Le Bocage twenty years ago. The Boston clientele was completely different—much more a steak and potatoes crowd.

I always tell people, if they want a good dinner, they should go to the restaurant on a week night, when the chef and waiter have time to do their jobs properly.

A good chef knows how to substitute. This soup could be made with zucchini, broccoli, lettuce—almost any ingredient...Fennel is an aromatic herb in the parsley family. It looks vaguely like celery and has the taste and aroma of anise.

RACK OF LAMB WITH POIVRADE SAUCE

3 racks lamb, trimed and
oven-ready
6 tablespoons melted butter

salt and pepper
POIVRADE SAUCE

1. Preheat oven to 425°
2. Brush the lamb with melted butter, season with salt and pepper and roast for 20 minutes or until cooked to taste. (Rare lamb will read 120° on a meat thermometer, medium-rare lamb—the way we like to serve it—will read 125°to 130°.) Let the meat rest for a few minutes before carving into chops.
3. Serve with Poivrade Sauce and a nice vegetable.

POIVRADE SAUCE

4 pounds lamb bones and
trimmings (shanks,
breasts and necks)
2 carrots, coarsely chopped
1 onion, peeled and
quartered
1 whole head garlic,
halved laterally
bouquet garni of bay leaf,
thyme and parsley
2½ quarts water
2 cups dry red wine

1 cup red wine vinegar
1 carrot, finely chopped
1 onion, peeled and chopped
2 shallots, chopped
3 sprigs parsley
2 teaspoons cracked
peppercorns
2 teaspoons potato starch
¼ cup Armagnac
1-2 teaspoons crème de cassis
(red currant liqueur)
salt and pepper

1. Preheat oven to 400°.
2. Roast bones for 1½ hours or until thoroughly browned. Drain off fat and transfer the bones to a stockpot with trimmings, coarsely chopped carrots, quartered onion, garlic, bouquet garni and water.
3. Bring to a boil, skim stock and reduce heat. Simmer for 5 hours, skimming from time to time to remove surface scum, adding more water as necessary to end up with 2 quarts lamb stock.

4. Strain into a saucepan, setting ¼ cup stock aside. Boil stock until reduced to about 2½ cups.

5. Place wine, vinegar, finely chopped carrot, chopped onion, shallots, parsley and cracked peppercorns in another saucepan and boil until reduced to about ½ cup.

6. Strain the wine reduction into the stock reduction and bring to a boil.

7. Dissolve the potato starch in the reserved ¼ cup lamb stock and whisk it into the boiling reduction to thicken.

8. Flame the Armagnac and add it to the sauce. Add the crème de cassis, which should impart a hint of fruit flavor to the sauce but not overpower it.

9. Correct the seasoning and strain the sauce through a fine sieve or cheesecloth before serving.

Note: You can use a good, homemade veal or chicken stock provided it's unsalted, but the flavor of the final sauce will not be the same. It always pays to keep a little extra stock on hand to adjust the sauce in case something does not go as planned.

Lamb is a young animal, so the difference between Prime and Choice is not that great. There is good lamb and bad lamb, however, and you should look for a light color and "large eye" when you do to select your rack. Unless you're an experienced meatcutter, have your butcher trim off the fat.

Armagnac is a grape brandy made in the southwest of France. We prefer it to Cognac for this dish, because long aging in wood makes it more flavorful. We use La Vie Armagnac, which is exceptionally good for the price.

GRATIN DAUPHINOISE

4 *Idaho potatoes, peeled and*
  cut into ¼" slices
1 *clove garlic, cut in half*
¼ *cup butter*

salt and butter
freshly grated nutmeg
1 *cup heavy cream*

1. Preheat oven to 350°
2. Place potato slices in cold, salted water to cover and bring to a boil. Check the potatoes after 2 to 3 minutes of boiling; if warm in the center, they are done. Drain thoroughly.
3. Rub a gratin or oven-proof baking dish with garlic and butter the dish liberally.
4. Arrange the potato slices in layers, sprinkling each layer with salt, pepper and nutmeg. There should be 2 to 3 layers.
5. Add enough heavy cream to cover. Bake the gratin for 1½ hours. The gratin is cooked when the cream is well reduced and drops of butter begin to form around the edge of the dish.

Note: This dish reheats well and should be cooked before the lamb goes into the oven.

You have to love this business. Small restaurants don't make millionaires. The restaurant has to be in your heart—you have to feel for it.

My wine steward is a gentleman, not a pressure guy. He loves wine—he's been studying wine ever since he came to work here. Why, he knows more about wine than I do!

PINEAPPLE WITH RUM

juice and grated rind of
  3 medium limes
2 ounces dark rum

1 large Hawaiian pineapple,
  peeled, cored and cut
  into large chunks

1. Place the pineapple chunks with reserved juices in a bowl and mix in the lime juice, rind and rum.
2. Chill for several hours in the refrigerator.
3. Serve the pineapple with its juice in wine or water goblets.

Skimping on the quality of the rum in this recipe will ruin the dessert. We use a dark rum called Myers's, which has lots of flavor.

Hawaiian pineapples are far superior to those of Texas. Hawaiian pineapples seem to be flavorful and ripe all year 'round. Don't waste your time on the Texas variety.

LEGAL SEA FOODS®

Dinner for Six

Stuffed Top Neck Clams

Fish Chowder

Steamed Haddock with Vegetables

Orange Sorbet Colada

Wines:

*With the Stuffed Clams and Chowder—Muscadet de Sèvre
et Maine Sur Lie (Louis Metaireau) 1977*

*With the Steamed Haddock—Johannisberg Riesling
(Ste. Michelle) 1978*

The Berkowitz Family, Proprietors

"If it isn't fresh, it isn't legal," is the motto of New England's premier seafood house, Legal Sea Foods. For three decades Legal's owners, the Berkowitz family, have been supplying Boston with its freshest seafood. The Berkowitzes sell a staggering twenty-seven tons of ocean-fresh fish weekly. Their newest restaurant alone serves 1,500 fish dinners a day.

Cambridge fish lovers fondly remember the first Legal Sea Foods restaurant, which opened in Inman Square in 1968. The fresh fish from the adjacent fish market was fried to order and served unceremoniously on paper plates with plastic cutlery. "In the beginning, our formula was to cut down on atmosphere and ambiance, to splurge on the food instead," recalls George Berkowitz. The formula worked wonders, for soon piscophiles from all over New England were waiting in block-long lines to savor the Legal seafood.

The sleek, new Legal's downtown has come a long way from the paper plates and picnic tables of the Inman Square eatery. "We also wanted a restaurant where people could dine more elegantly," says Roger Berkowitz, who runs the downtown Legal's. So when space became available in the former Terrace Room of the Park Plaza Hotel last January, the Berkowitzes leapt at the opportunity to launch their third Legal Sea Foods restaurant. Canvas hangings, brass railings and a soft blue and white color scheme create a maritime atmosphere at the new Legal's. The bright, multi-tiered dining area, suggesting the decks of a stately ship, seats 200, with room for seventy-five more in the lounge.

The Legal's system, with its rotating servers and pay-when-you-order policy, perplexes newcomers to the restaurant. "Unlike most restaurants, we refuse to hold one dish under a heat lamp until the entire order is ready," Roger Berkowitz explains. "As soon as a dish is ready, it is served by the first available waitress. To us at Legal Sea Foods, protocol is second to taste."

The Boston Park Plaza
43 Boylston Street
426-4444

STUFFED TOP NECK CLAMS

12 *live top neck or cherrystone clams, well scrubbed*
1 *small onion, finely chopped*
1 *stalk celery, finely choped*
½ *green pepper, cored, seeded and finely chopped*
2 *tablespoons butter*
2 *tablespoons finely chopped parsley*

1 *cup dry white wine*
¾ *cup dried bread crumbs*
1 *tablespoon Dijon-style mustard*
  salt and freshly ground black pepper
½ *cup toasted, slivered almonds*

1. Preheat oven to 450°.
2. Place clams in a saucepan with ¼ inch of water and steam, covered, until shells open. Remove the clams from the shells and chop, reserving shell bottoms.
3. Strain and reserve the clam broth.
4. Sauté the onion, celery and green pepper in butter until soft. Stir in the parsley, wine, bread crumbs, mustard and chopped clams. Add enough of the clam broth to make a moist stuffing. Season to taste.

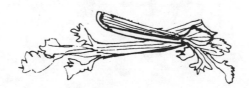

5. Divide the clam stuffing evenly among the reserved shells and top with toasted almonds. (The stuffed clams can be prepared ahead of time to this point.)

6. Bake for 15 minutes and serve at once.

Top neck clams are a little smaller than cherrystones and are more flavorful. Do not use quahogs—clams with shells larger than 3 inches—they are too tough.

FISH CHOWDER

2 onions, finely chopped
2 leeks, white part only,
   finely chopped
¼ cup butter
4 potatoes, peeled and diced
   salt and freshly ground
   black pepper

2 cups boiling water or
   FISH STOCK (see index)
1 pound mixed cod and
   flounder
3 cups light cream
½ cup grated Swiss cheese

1. Sauté the onions and leeks in butter until soft. Add the potatoes, salt, pepper and water or fish stock and bring to a boil.
2. Layer the fish on top of the vegetables, reduce heat and simmer the chowder, covered, for 30 minutes.
3. Add the light cream and warm, but do not boil. Correct the seasoning.
4. To serve, ladle the chowder into oven-proof soup bowls and sprinkle with grated cheese. Place in a very hot oven or under the broiler and cook until the cheese is melted and golden. Serve immediately.

There is no need to add flour to this fish chowder—the potatoes act as a thickener in themselves.

"Fresh fish" is a misnomer at most restaurants. All it means, technically, is that the fish has not been frozen. Fish caught the first day of a ten-day fishing trip is not very fresh by our standards.

STEAMED HADDOCK WITH VEGETABLES

6 (9-ounce) pieces of
   fillet of haddock
6 carrots, peeled and cut
   into ¼"x¼"x2" sticks
1½ pounds zucchini, thinly
   sliced
1½ pounds broccoli, florets only

1 pound straw or regular
   mushrooms, washed and
   quartered
3 tablespoons butter
12 thin slices tomato
1½ pounds mild Cheddar
   cheese, grated

1. Preheat oven to 450°.
2. Overlap 2 sheets of 12-inch by 16-inch aluminum foil on a work surface to form a 12-inch by 19-inch rectangle. Place a piece of haddock in the center. Arrange one-sixth of the carrots, zucchini, broccoli and mushrooms in small piles around the fish, alternating colors. Dot the fish and vegetables with butter. Place two slices of tomato on top of the fish and sprinkle a handful of cheese on top. Fold the flaps of foil over the fish and seal the top and edges to form a tent around the filling. Make five more fish-vegetable tents following this procedure.
3. Bake fish bundles for 35 to 40 minutes. Open one bundle to make sure the fish is cooked—it should pull apart easily in moist flakes. For serving, slash the foil along the bottom and slide fish and vegetables onto warm dinner plates.

Truly fresh fish will not have a fishy smell. When you run your finger along a fillet of fresh fish, nothing should come off.

When fish is cooked, its translucent grey color will turn white. The flesh should come apart in moist flakes.

ORANGE SORBET COLADA

½ cup plus 2 tablespoons
   white rum
½ cup plus 2 tablespoons
   triple sec
3 tablespoons grenadine

1½ cups fresh orange juice
1 (12-ounce) can
   piña colada mix
3 cups crushed ice
1 orange, thinly sliced

Place all ingredients except orange slices in a blender and churn for 45 seconds or until the colada is of soft serving consistance. (You may need to do it in 2 batches for this quantity.) Pour into chilled 12-ounce wine glasses and garnish with orange slices for serving.

L'espalier

Dinner for Six

Bay Scallops à la Nage

Lamb Noisettes with Onions and Mint

Bing Cherry Clafoutis

Wines:

With the Lamb—Château Malartic-Lagravière Graves 1971

With the Scallops—Vouvray Sec (Clos du Bourg) 1974

Moncef Meddeb, Proprietor and Chef
Dona Doll, Proprietor

Y ou don't have to tell Moncef Meddeb about the rigors and privations of the restaurant trade. Six days a week the indefatigable owner of L'Espalier on Gloucester Street spends fifteen hours on his feet, handpicking the day's produce, butchering his own meats, simmering his stocks and sauces, cooking each and every dinner to order and tasting it before it goes out to the dining room. "I wonder if I have all my sanity, sometimes," he muses, "but then there are the high moments, when my cooking attains a little piece of Truth and that's what keeps me going."

Truth is a pretty high-minded ideal for the restaurant business, but then L'Espalier is no common place restaurant. L'Espalier's namesake—a pear tree trimmed and trained to grow in perfect symmetry—serves as an apt symbol for the restaurant's cuisine: the transformation of nature's finest ingredients into something considerably more sophisticated and refined. The menu, which varies daily, offers a felicitous blend of nouvelle and classical French cuisine. "We cause ourselves extra hardship by changing the menu so often," Moncef concedes, "but the reality of the fish and produce out there changes daily, too." With twelve cooks and fifty-five seats in the dining room, L'Espalier has one of the highest chef to client ratios in Boston. "Without the extra hands, we just couldn't serve the kind of food we believe in," Moncef says.

A Tunisian by birth, Moncef Meddeb grew up outside Paris, where his parents raised vegetables, fruit trees and rabbits. His cooking reflects his dual heritage in his fondness for the bold flavors of North Africa and his dovotion to the classicism of France. In 1978, Moncef and Dona Doll purchased the former Dodin Bouffant on Boylston Street where Moncef quickly distinguished himself. The restaurant has since moved to Gloucester Street where it occupies the first two floors of a Victorian town house. Here clients wait in a salon with a fireplace to be seated either in the high-ceilinged downstairs parlor with its French stucco and ornate mantlepiece or upstairs where stuffed birds and period canvases lend the charm of an English hunting lodge.

384 Boylston Street
262-3023

BAY SCALLOPS À LA NAGE

18 snow peas pods
⅔ cup freshly shucked
    sweet peas
2 large tomatoes
1 teaspoon freshly
    grated orange peel
1 quart boiling water

COURT BOUILLON
1½ pounds Bay, Cape or small
    sea scallops
½ teaspoon sherry vinegar
5⅓ tablespoons unsalted butter
    salt and freshly ground
    Szechuan peppercorns

1. Preheat oven to 150°.
2. Plunge the snow peas into boiling, salted water for 2 minutes. Remove with slotted spoon, rinse under cold water, drain and set aside. Plunge sweet peas into same boiling, salted water, drain and set aside.
3. To peel and seed the tomatoes, slash an "x" on the bottom of each tomato, plunge into boiling water for 10 seconds, rinse under cold water and slip of the skins. Cut tomatoes in half widthwise and wring out the seeds and pulp with the palm of your hand.
4. Place the orange peel in a strainer and pour 1 quart of boiling water over it.
5. Strain the Court Bouillon, reserving the vegetables, and bring to a boil. Add the scallops (small half-moon muscle removed from the sides) and cook for 2 minutes. Remove the scallops with a slotted spoon and divide evenly among six serving bowls. Keep warm in oven.
6. Reduce the Court Bouillon at a rapid boil for 2 minutes and add the sherry vinegar. Whisk in the butter rapidly, followed by the snow peas, fresh peas, tomatoes, orange peel and a few of the vegetables reserved from the strained Court Bouillon.
7. Remove from heat and season to taste. Ladle the nage over the scallops and serve at once.

Nager *is the French word for "swim." The scallops* à la nage *in this recipe do their swimming in a spicy broth.*

COURT BOUILLON

6 cups water
2 carrots, peeled and
   thinly sliced
1 leek, white part only,
   washed and thinly sliced
8 small white onions, peeled
   and thinly sliced
2 shallots, peeled and
   thinly sliced

cheesecloth spice bag:
  2 unpeeled cloves garlic
  2 strips lemon peel
  1 clove
  1 bay leaf
  pinch of thyme
  sprig of parsley
  ½ teaspoon fennel seeds
1 cup dry white wine

1. Combine all ingredients except the wine in a large pot and simmer for 30 minutes.
2. Add the wine, bring the broth just to a boil and remove from heat. Discard the cheesecloth spice bag and cool.

Note: This makes five and one-half cups.

Court Bouillon means "brief broth," literally, referring to the fact that water has been used to prepare this poaching liquid, instead of the customary, long-simmered fish stock.

FRESH SWEET PEAS

1½ cups freshly shucked
   sweet peas
1 quart boiling, salted water

¼ cup unsalted butter
salt and pepper

1. Plunge peas into boiling, salted water and cook for 3 minutes. Rinse peas under cold running water to fix the color and drain.
2. Just prior to serving, melt the butter in a sauté pan and cook peas for 2 to 3 more minutes or until tender. Season with salt and pepper and serve.

LAMB NOISETTES WITH ONION AND MINT

2 large onions, peeled
   and quartered
1 quart lamb stock
¼ cup heavy cream
   salt, pepper, freshly
   grated nutmeg
1 tablespoon olive oil
½ cup unsalted butter

6 (6-ounce) lamb noisettes
   (thick steaks cut from the
   loin or tenderloin)
2 shallots, minced
2 tablespoons sherry
   wine vinegar
2 tablespoons meat glaze
12 fresh mint leaves
   FRESH SWEET PEAS

1. Preheat oven to 450°.

2. Simmer the onions in lamb stock until very, very soft. Remove onions with a slotted spoon and purée in a food processor or blender. Set aside the onion-flavored stock.

3. Transfer the onion purée to a heavy saucepan and simmer for a few minutes to evaporate most of the moisture. Add the heavy cream and simmer for a few more minutes. Season with salt, pepper and nutmeg. Set aside and keep warm.

4. Heat the olive oil with 2 tablespoons butter in a sauté pan and sear the lamb noisettes on all sides. Finish cooking the lamb on a hot broiling pan in the oven for 10 to 12 minutes for medium rare or to taste. When the lamb is cooked as desired, remove it from the oven and let it rest for 2 minutes.

5. Meanwhile, discard all but 1 teaspoon fat in the sauté pan and add the shallots. Cook the shallots for 30 seconds or until lightly browned. Deglaze the pan with the sherry vinegar and simmer until most of the liquid has evaporated. Add the stock and continue simmering until 1 cup liquid remains. Whisk in the meat glaze and correct the seasoning. Set aside and keep warm.

6. Warm six large dinner plates. Mince the mint leaves and stir them into the onion purée. Whisk the remaining butter into the hot sauce in little pieces.

7. Thinly slice the lamb noisettes and fan out the pieces at the top of each plate. Spoon the onion purée onto the center of each plate and sprinkle with the Fresh Sweet Peas. Ladle the sauce around the edge of each plate, not over the lamb or onion, and serve the noisettes at once.

BING CHERRY CLAFOUTIS

3 cups fresh Bing or black
   cherries, pitted and
   stems removed
½ cup kirschwasser
¾ cup heavy cream

2 whole eggs
6 tablespoons sugar
   orange blossom water
1 9" pie shell made with
   PÂTE ROYALE

1. Soak the cherries in the kirschwasser for 1 hour.
2. Preheat oven to 400°.
3. Blend the cream, eggs and sugar together, adding a few drops orange blossom water for flavor.
4. Drain the cherries and arrange in a pre-baked pie shell. Pour the egg mixture over the cherries and bake in oven for 20 minutes or until an inserted skewer comes out clean. Serve either warm or cold.

Note: Orange blossom water—a fragrant, perfumy flavoring—is available in most Middle Eastern or Armenian markets.

PÂTE ROYALE

1 cup unsalted butter	1½ teaspoons sugar
2 cups all-purpose white flour	2 egg yolks
1 teaspoon salt	3 tablespoons heavy cream

1. Preheat oven to 375°.

2. Cut the butter finely into the flour and turn out onto a flat work surface. Make a well in the butter-flour mixture and place the remaining ingredients in the center. Mix the liquid ingredients with the fingertips, gradually incorporating the flour, and knead with the heel of the palm to obtain a smooth dough. Work the dough as little as possible. Chill dough for at least 30 minutes before rolling it out.

3. Tap the dough with a rolling pin to soften it and roll dough out to a ⅜-inch thickness. Line a 9-inch pie pan with the dough and chill for 10 minutes. (You will probably have a little dough left over—use it to make little cookies.)

4. Prick the bottom of the pie shell with a fork and line with a sheet of parchment paper or tinfoil. Fill the pie shell with rice. (This helps the dough hold its shape while baking.)

5. Bake the lined tart shell for 20 minutes. Remove the rice and paper and continue baking for 5 to 7 minutes to dry out the bottom of the crust.

If you're in the restaurant business to make money—with a fine restaurant, at least—you probably ought to try another profession…You have to have a generous nature in your cooking. I am both the owner and the chef of L'Espalier. More often than not, it's the chef who dictates the expenditures.

LOCKE-OBER CAFE

EST.-1875

WINTER PLACE

Dinner for Four

Oysters à la Gino

Lobster Stew

Breast of Chicken Sauté à la Richmond

Belgian Endive Salad with House Dressing

Indian Pudding

Wines:

With the Oysters—Johannisberg Riesling
(Rutherford Hill) 1978

With the Chicken—Chardonnay (San Martin) 1978

With the Pudding—Lake County Muscat Canelli
(Fetzer) 1978

Jeff Sullivan, General Manager

Boston has changed a lot since 1875 when Louis Ober opened his Restaurant Parisien at 4 Winter Place. However, at his legacy—the Locke-Ober Café—time has stood still. Guests still dine amid the splendor of the Gay '90s—the gold-leaf wallpaper and hand-carved Dominican mahogany woodwork; the gleaming silver steam tables and bronze *Gloria Victis,* a statue which doubles as a hat rack; the rose nude portrait of Mademoiselle Yvonne, to whom generations of bon vivants have raised toasts. It is true that ten years ago "ladies" dared to cross the threshold of Locke-Ober's hallowed Men's Bar on the ground floor. Despite the architectural and social upheavals which have swept the rest of Boston, the Locke-Ober Café has remained much as it was when it opened over a century ago.

It is often said that fine food and vintage wine are a heaven-made marriage. The initial union of Frank Locke's Wine Rooms and Louis Ober's Restaurant Parisien, however, was anything but felicitous. Frank Locke, a retired sea captain, spurned the fancy French fare of his Winter Place neighbor and set up shop next door to Ober's place in 1891, purveying hard liquor, Maine lobster and solid steak and potatoes. In time the public came to prefer Locke's for drinking, but Ober's for dining, and would file from one establishment to the other through a narrow door which joined them.

The competition ended in 1894, when a liquor company purchased both restaurants. The key to the door which separated them was ceremoniously tossed into the Boston Harbor and the modern Locke-Ober's was born. A Frenchman, Emile Camus, who reigned over 4 Winter Place for the next forty-five years, undertook the task of uniting the restaurants. To this day, Locke-Ober's bill of fare combines the extravagance of Ober's continental cuisine with the hardy Yankee cooking of the Maine sea captain, Locke.

Restaurant manager Jeff Sullivan remarks, "Many of our waiters have been here for forty years." In 1980 the restaurant underwent a few tasteful alterations in keeping with its character, including the addition of a plush bar on the first floor.

4 Winter Place
542-1340

OYSTERS À LA GINO

2 cloves garlic, peeled
12 lean strips bacon
2 cups fresh crab meat
4 teaspoons paprika
1¼ cups CREAM SAUCE
¼ cup Madeira wine

salt and freshly ground
  black pepper
1½ cups fresh bread crumbs
¼ cup olive oil
rock salt
24 large oysters,
  freshly opened
lemon wedges

1. Preheat oven to 375°.
2. Mince one clove garlic with four strips bacon and fry until the bacon is crisp. Pour off fat. Blend the bacon-garlic mixture with the crab meat and 2 teapoons paprika. Fold in Cream Sauce, wine, salt and pepper. Bring to a quick boil, pour into a shallow pan and cool.
3. Mince the remaining garlic and mix with bread crumbs, remaining paprika and olive oil.
4. Cover four oven-proof plates with a ¼-inch layer of rock salt and place six large oysters on the half shell on each plate. Spoon a generous mound of the crab meat mixture on each oyster, then sprinkly on a layer of bread crumbs.
5. Cut remaining bacon strips in thirds. Top each oyster with a curled piece of raw bacon.
6. Bake for 15 minutes or until the bacon is crisp and the crumb topping is brown. Serve at once with lemon wedges.

Chef Gino Bertolacconi invented this dish thirty years ago while experimenting with Oysters Rockefeller.

CREAM SAUCE

6 tablespoons butter
6 tablespoons flour
1½ cups milk

1½ cups light cream
    pinch of salt

1. Melt butter over a double boiler, stir in flour and let cook for 10 minutes.
2. Scald milk and cream in a separate pan and whisk gradually into the butter-flour mixture.
3. Add salt and cook slowly for 45 minutes, stirring from time to time.

Note: This makes about three cups. Use remainder for the chicken.

LOBSTER STEW

1½ pounds cooked lobster
    meat, diced
½ cup unsalted butter
    tomalley from the lobster
1 teaspoon paprika

2 cups light cream
2 cups milk
   salt and freshly ground
   black pepper

1. Gently sauté the lobster in 6 tablespoons butter in a 2-quart saucepan for 3 to 4 minutes or until the meat is firm. Add the tomalley and paprika and sauté briefly.
2. Pour in the cream and milk and heat thoroughly, but do not let boil. Season to taste and ladle into a soup tureen.
3. Float the remaining butter on top and serve immediately with pilot crackers.

Note: Some people like to add Tabasco or Worcestershire sauce, but this should be left to the diner's discretion.

When John F. Kennedy lunched at Locke-Ober's, he would invariably order the Lobster Stew. "The broth is for me," he would say and give his waiter the lobster meat.

BREAST OF CHICKEN SAUTÉ Á LA RICHMOND

6 tablespoons butter
4 boned chicken breasts
12 medium-size
     mushroom caps
¾ cup sherry
¾ cup light cream

4 (¼" thick) slices
     of cooked ham
   CREAM SAUCE
   salt and pepper
4 slices white bread,
     trimmed and toasted

1. Preheat oven to 350°.
2. Melt half the butter in a large sauté pan and add the chicken, skin side down. Sauté for 5 minutes or until golden brown. Turn the breasts and add the mushroom caps. Cook for 5 minutes, pour off fat and add half the sherry, half the cream, the ham, the Cream Sauce and the seasonings. Cover and bake for 30 minutes.
3. Place a piece of toast in each of four shirred egg dishes or individual au gratin dishes. Remove ham, chicken and mushrooms from sauce; arrange ham slices on top of toast, chicken breasts on top of ham and divide the mushroom caps evenly among the dishes. Whisk the remaining sherry, cream and butter into the sauce left in the pan and simmer for 3 minutes. Strain sauce over chicken.
4. Cover each dish with a *sous cloche* (glass bell) and place in a hot oven until the condensation under the glass clears. If you do not have glass bells, omit this step and serve at once.

Note: This dish would be really nice with a smoked ham, like Smithfield ham. If you use smoked ham, it should be very thinly sliced.

Locke-Ober's is an institution, you see. We don't try to compete with other restaurants. We try to stay with the dishes which made Locke-Ober's great to begin with. If someone wants something that's not on our menu and we have the ingredients, we'll be glad to make it . We want people to really feel at home at Locke-Ober's.

BELGIAN ENDIVE SALAD WITH HOUSE DRESSING

4 large leaves Boston lettuce
4 stalks Belgian endive,
    cut into large strips

4 large pieces canned
    hearts of palm, quartered
4 small cooked beets, diced
1 cup HOUSE DRESSING

1. Cover four chilled salad plates with lettuce leaves.
2. Place a bundle of endive in the center of each plate. Garnish with hearts of palm pieces and beets.
3. Spoon the House Dressing over the salad for serving.

HOUSE DRESSING

⅔ teaspoon salt
¼ teaspoon paprika
⅓ teaspoon dry mustard
⅓ teaspoon white pepper
    juice of ½ lemon
4 tablespoons cider vinegar
1 clove garlic, crushed

¾ cup olive oil
1 tablespoon finely
    chopped pimiento
1 tablespoon chopped fresh
    green pepper
1½ teaspoons chopped parsley
1½ teaspoons chopped
    scallions

Combine all of the ingredients in a large jar and shake to mix thoroughly.

Note: The dressing must be shaken directly before pouring over the salad.

INDIAN PUDDING

¼ cup corn meal	¼ cup sugar
2 cups cold milk	½ teaspoon cinnamon
2 cups scalded milk	½ teaspoon ginger
½ cup molasses	4 tablespoons butter
1 teaspoon salt	2 tablespoons white rum

1. Preheat oven to 250°.
2. Mix the corn meal with enough cold milk to pour easily. Stir until smooth. Slowly add the scalded milk and cook over a double boiler for 20 minutes or until the mixture thickens.
3. Add the molasses, salt, sugar, cinnamon, ginger and butter and pour into a buttered pudding dish. Pour the remaining cold milk and rum over the pudding.
4. Set the dish in a pan of hot water and bake for 3 hours. Let stand ½ hour before serving.

This is one our most famous dishes. It should be served with a scoop of vanilla ice cream.

A good chef is someone who works his way up through the ranks. Most of our employees have worked their way up. Even our chef came here as a dishwasher. A good chef is someone who, no matter how much he knows, is always willing to listen, to try something a new way. He is someone who is proud of his product, who is willing to please, who can get along with other people.

maison robert

Dinner for Four

Potage Santé

Terrine de Poireaux au Coulis de Tomates

Estouffade de Lotte au Muscadet

Céleris Braises

Tarte Tatin

Wines:

With the Meal—Muscadet sur Lie Cuvée de Prestige
(L. Metaireau) 1977-78

With the Tarte Tatin—Château Roumieu-Lacoste 1975

Ann and Lucien Robert, Proprietors
Pierre Jamet and Phillipe Gareau, Chefs

"Opening another restaurant was the last thing we had in mind," recall Ann and Lucien Robert, proprietors of the prestigious Maison Robert. But when space became available in the freshly renovated Old City Hall in 1972, the pair could not resist the stately, historic setting for a new dining establishment. Built in 1865, Old City Hall remains one of the finest examples of French Second Empire architecture in North America—in the Roberts' minds the perfect foil for Lucien's classiacal French cuisine.

Maison Robert is actually two restaurants. The elegant Bonhomme Richard offers formal French dining amid the high ceilings, oak paneling and serene view of King's Chapel of the former City Treasurer's office. The tastefully appointed Ben's Café in the old City Vault downstairs may be less formal, though no less elegant. The two restaurants, private dining rooms and outdoor terrace combined seat 300.

Both Bonhomme Richard and Ben's Café—named for Benjamin Franklin, whose statue graces Maison Robert's portals—serve impeccably prepared classical French cuisine. "Our chefs are free to experiment, but not on the customers," says Lucien Robert. "Every dish is tasted by my wife, my staff and me before we consider putting it on the menu." A full-time kitchen staff of twenty-five, a quarter of which are French, help Monsieur Robert uphold the quality and authenticity of his fare.

The son of farmer, Lucien Robert was born in Normandy and trained at some of the top restaurants in Paris, including Prunier and the Pavillon D'Armenomville, before coming to the United States in 1951. A year-long visit became a life-long sojourn when the young chef met his future wife Ann, a historian in Madison, Wisconsin. Drawn by the rich cultural heritage of the Bay State, they settled in Boston in 1953. Maison Robert is Lucien's third French restaurant in the city and the crowning achievement of a busy, ambitious career.

45 School Street
227-3370

POTAGE SANTÉ
Sorrel Soup

2 large leeks, white part only, sliced lengthwise	1 quart chicken consommé
4 tablespoons butter	½ pound fresh sorrel leaves
4 medium-size potatoes, peeled and quartered	2 egg yolks
	1 cup heavy cream
	salt and pepper

1. Chop the leeks and lightly sauté in 2 tablespoons butter. Add the potatoes and consommé and boil rapidly for 10 minutes or until potatoes are cooked.
2. Transfer potatoes and leeks to a blender or food processor and purée. Recombine the purée with broth.
3. Wash the sorrel and remove stems. Sauté for 2 to 3 minutes in the remaining butter. Finely chop the cooked sorrel and add it to the soup.
4. Heat the soup to a simmer and mix the yolks with the cream. Little by little, whisk 1 cup of the soup into the yolk-cream mixture, then stir this back into the soup.
5. Gently warm the soup to cook the egg yolks and thicken the soup—do not let boil or the soup will curdle. Season to taste. Serve with fresh butter-fried croutons.

We only put Potage Santé on our menu when we have enough fresh sorrel in our garden to make it. We always serve salmon with fresh sorrel in the summertime.

Like most dreams in life, mine has been difficult to obtain. To produce a perfect meal or perfect service…it rarely happens. The restaurant business is very challenging and every day the challenge begins anew.

As a fellow restaurateur in town here says, "I'm just as good as the last meal I cooked." It's a marvelous and humble way to express the truth of the restaurant business…Our long-term goals for the restaurant are very simple: always to be better, and to have fun trying.

TERRINE DE POIREAUX AU COULIS DE TOMATES
Terrine of Leeks with a Fresh Tomato Sauce

20 leeks, white part only,
   sliced to the root lengthwise
1 quart beef consommé

2 envelopes gelatin,
   softened in ½ cup water
salt and pepper
COULIS DE TOMATES

1. Tie the leeks into bundles and cook in boiling, salted water until tender. Refresh under cold running water and drain well.
2. Heat consommé until hot.
3. Melt the softened gelatin over a pan of boiling water and stir it into the hot consommé. Season to taste.
4. Cool the consommé until it is thick and oily and on the verge of setting. Dip each individual leek in the consommé and place in a 1½-quart terrine mold, pour the remaining consommé over them. Refrigerate overnight.
5. To serve, cut into ½-inch slices with a sharp knife. Serve the Coulis de Tomates on the side.

Consistency is the most important ingredient for running a restaurant successfully. If you are consistent, you clients will never be disappointed.

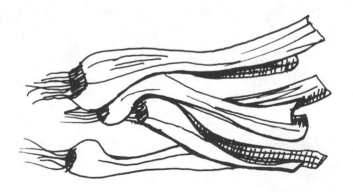

MAISON ROBERT

COULIS DE TOMATES

3 large ripe tomatoes
¼ cup red wine vinegar
¼ cup virgin olive oil

¼ cup chopped parsley
salt and freshly ground
black pepper

1. To peel the tomatoes, cut a small "x" on the bottoms, plunge into boiling water for 10 seconds, rinse under cold water and slip off skins.
2. Halve the tomatoes widthwise and wring out the seed and pulp with the palm of your hand.
3. Chop the tomatoes very finely and whisk in the remaining ingredients. Correct the season before serving.

Note: This recipe will serve eight to ten people.

ESTOUFFADE DE LOTTE AU MUSCADET
Monkfish Cooked in Muscadet Wine

2 shallots, minced
6 tablespoons butter
1 leek, white part only,
   thinly sliced
1 carrot, peeled and
   finely diced

1½ pounds trimmed monkfish,
   cut into 1"cubes
2 cups Muscadet wine
¾ cup whipping cream
1 cup seedless white grapes,
   peeled

1. Gently sauté shallots in 3 tablespoons butter. Stir in the chopped leek and carrot and continue sautéing until the vegetables are soft, but not browned.
2. Add the monkfish and gently sauté over medium heat for 3 minutes, shaking the pan to thoroughly mix the fish with the vegetables.
3. Pour in the wine and bring almost to a boil. Remove pan from heat, cover and allow the fish to poach in the hot broth for 6 to 7 minutes.
4. Remove the fish and vegetables from the poaching liquid with a slotted spoon and transfer to a warm platter. Bring the broth to a boil and cook until only 3 to 4 tablespoons liquid remain.
5. Remove pan from heat and whisk in the remaining butter and whipping cream. Warm this sauce over a low heat, but do not let boil or it will curdle.
6. Add the peeled grapes to the sauce to warm, then pour the sauce over the monkfish and vegetables. Serve at once.

Note: Monkfish—sometimes called goosefish or angler—can be found at gourmet seafood shops and ethnic fishmongers. Be sure to trim away the wet, purplish membrane before using.

We were the first restaurant in Boston to serve lotte—*monkfish. In this country it's considered a trash fish, though in France it's deemed a delicacy. So we would have our monkfish specially flown in from France., Eventually we learned that American fishermen were selling the monkfish they caught here to the French, so the* lotte *which appeared on our menu had crossed the Atlantic twice!*

CÉLERIS BRAISES
Braised Celery

2 bunches celery
½ cup unsalted butter
½ clove garlic, minced
½ small onion, finely chopped
1 carrot, finely diced

½ bay leaf
2 cups veal stock
 salt and pepper
¼ cup heavy cream

1. Preheat oven to 350°.
2. Remove the tops and bottoms of the celery and cut stalks in 6-inch lengths. Peel the rounded sides of the stalks with a vegetable peeler to remove the strings. Blanch the celery in boiling water for 3 minutes, rinse in cold water and drain.
3. Melt the butter in a deep pan. When it foams, add the celery pieces and brown on all sides. Add all remaining ingredients except the cream and cover. Cook over a low heat or in preheated oven until celery is very tender—about 40 to 50 minutes.
4. Transfer the celery to a lightly buttered, oven-proof serving dish and pour over it a few tablespoons of the cooking liquid, plus the heavy cream. Bake for 5 more minutes before serving.

My advice to someone who wants to open a restaurant? First, prepare yourself and thoroughly learn the business. Second, take pride in what you do and do it well. Finally, forget about the cash register...Too many restaurateurs are too busy counting their money. If you do a good job, the cash register will show it in the long run. Quality or profit doesn't have to be an either/or matter. If you really apply yourself, you can have both.

TARTE TATIN
Upside-Down Apple Pie

1 cup, plus 2 tablespoons
   unsalted butter
1½ cups sugar

20 Golden Delicious apples,
    peeled, cored and halved
   juice of 1 lemon
   PÂTE BRISÉE

1. Preheat oven to 375°.
2. Smear a tarte tatin mold or 16-inch cast iron frying pan with the butter and sprinkle with the sugar. Arrange the apple halves in the mold in overlapping spirals—they should be quite closely packed together—and sprinkle with lemon juice. Cook the apples over a medium flame until the sugar caramelizes and the bottoms of the apples turn a golden brown.
3. Remove from heat and cover the top of the pan with a circle of Pâte Brisée rolled to a thickness of ⅜-inch. Bake the tart for 1 hour.
4. Remove from the oven and place a round serving platter on top. Invert the frying pan without delay—the tart should slide easily from the mold.

Note: Serve warm with créme fraîche or whipped cream on the side.

My first advice for making Tarte Tatin is to completely line the top of your stove with tin foil before starting. That way, when the tart spatters, you won't spend your whole night cleaning your stove top!

MAISON ROBERT

PÂTE BRISÉE

1 cup, less 2 tablespoons
    butter
2½ cups flour

¼ cup sugar
    pinch of salt
½ cup cold water

Cut the butter into the flour with a pastry cutter. Add the sugar and salt to the water and blend lightly with the flour-butter mixture. Gently knead the dough into a ball. Chill for at least 2 hours before rolling out into desired round shape.

The recipe for this Tarte Tatin was brought to us by a visiting chef from Nantes. It has become one of the most poular desserts on our menu. We make our tarts fresh every noon and evening. Our Tarte Tatin has never seen the inside of the refrigerator.

Panache

Dinner for Four

Warmed Scallops with Coriander

Sautéed Duck Panache

Green Beans with Garlic

Tangerine Mousse

Wine:

Corton-Charlemagne Diamond Jubilee
(Remoissenet Père et Fils) 1971

Bruce Frankel, Proprietor and Chef

Bruce Frankel did not set out to become the iconoclast of the Boston food scene, but his restaurant Panache has been at the center of controversy since it opened in January 1979. The young restaurateur baffled the critics with his unusual flavor combinations and small, nouvelle cuisine-sized portions. The public quickly recognized in Frankel, however, one of the most innovative and important of the Hub's new wave of chefs.

It's no accident people find a Zen-like quality in the Panache dining experience. For years Frankel adhered to a strict macrobiotic diet—a regimen of "controlled starvation," he recalls, which forced him to sharpen his culinary creativity. From there it was on to French cuisine, working at several Back Bay restaurants, where Frankel learned the classical foundations of cooking, plus an ever-evolving repertory of flavors and techniqes. Oriental, European and American influences come together in Frankel's current creations—the fruits of what he calls a "highly stylized, highly personal cuisine."

The decor of Panache is a deliberate exercise in understatement and good taste. The casually elegant and chic restaurant, which recently underwent a facelift, is done in greys, pinks, and burgundies. Graceful armchairs, sprays of silk flowers and French menues and Japanese prints on the walls add to the elán at Panache—a name meaning "a plume of feathers" and, by extension, anything with bravado, swagger and verve.

"I guess I'm a radical in the truest sense of the word," says Frankel. "I'm trying to get to the roots of cooking. I've discarded all superfluities, like liveried waiters or garnishes you can't eat. I think that people would rather taste an interesting sauce, than one that is technically correct."

798 Main Street
Cambridge
492-9500

WARMED SCALLOPS WITH CORIANDER

12 ounces fresh Bay or
    Cape scallops
3 branches fresh coriander
6 cups FISH STOCK
    (see index)
    or bottled clam juice
2 small shallots,
    very finely chopped

salt
12 coarse grinds of
    Szechuan peppercorns
1 tablespoon raspberry
    vinegar
1 tablespoon peanut oil
2 tablespoon walnut oil

1. Remove the half-moon-shaped muscle on the side of each scallop, then cut scallops horizontally into ¼-inch slices.
2. Pluck the coriander leaves from the stems, rinse in cold water, then dry between paper towels.
3. Slightly oversalt the Fish Stock (but not the clam juice) and heat to simmer.
4. Combine shallots, salt, Szechuan peppercorns and vinegar in a small mixing bowl and whisk in both oils drop by drop to obtain a rich emulsion. Taste and correct the seasoning.
5. Place scallops in a strainer and immerse in hot Fish Stock for 30 seconds. Drain the scallops thoroughly on paper towel and divide evenly among four warm plates.
6. Sprinkle coriander leaves on top and pour the dressing over the scallops. Pat the scallops gently with your fingertips to mix in the dressing. Serve while still warm.

This dish is an excellent example of nouvelle cuisine. It utilizes many of the "new" ingredients, a radical cooking technique, and a simple but stiking presentation.

To me, nouvelle cuisine is the forefront of the evolution of cooking. No one is adding new dishes to Chinese or Hungarian cuisine. The French are regarded as the Establishment of the food world and yet they are coming out with this exciting new cuisine. Nouvelle cuisine is not some trendy little thing dreamed up by some bunch of kids; its advocates and pioneer are the most serious chefs in France.

SAUTÉED DUCK PANACHE

2 (4 to 6 pound) ducks
    salt and freshly ground
      white pepper to taste
    DUCK STOCK
1 tablespoon granulated
    sugar

1 tablespoon sherry vinegar
¼ cup dry white wine
¼ teaspoon grated lemon rind
½ cup cold unsalted butter,
    cut into ¼" pieces

1. Preheat oven to 350°.
2. Use a sharp boning knife to remove the leg-thigh sections from each duck. Trim away all visible fat and all but a one inch border of skin and chop off the last ½-inch of the drumstick. Remove the breast halves from each duck by cutting along the breastbone and rib cage and trim all fat and sinewy membranes from the meat.
3. Place a large cast-iron frying pan over a medium flame and when the pan is hot, add the duck legs skin side down. Reduce heat. Salt and pepper the legs and fry for 10 minutes. Turn the legs and cook the meat side for only 3 minutes. Turn again and continue cooking until the skin is nicely browned and crispy.
4. Transfer the legs to a large to a roasting pan and bake for 30 minutes.
5. Meanwhile, place Duck Stock in a wide saucepan and boil until only 1 cup remains.
6. Place a small frying pan over a medium flame and when the pan is hot, sprinkle in the sugar. Cook until it caramelizes, but do not let burn.
7. Remove caramel from heat and pour in the vinegar and wine to deglaze the pan. (Be careful: the mixture will sputter and sizzle.) You may need to stir the mixture with a whisk to completely dissolve the sugar.
8. Add the lemon rind and stock reduction. Simmer this mixture to obtain a consistency of light cream. Lower the heat and add the butter piece by piece, gently swirling the pan.
9. Correct the seasoning with salt and pepper, strain sauce through a fine sieve and reserve over warm water.

10. Remove duck legs from oven when done and pour off fat, reserving ¼-inch. Cut legs at the joint and drain on paper towels. Keep warm.

11. Reheat the frying pan with the duck fat and cook the duck breasts 3 minutes per side for medium rare. Sprinkle with salt and pepper while cooking.

12. Pour the sauce onto four warm plates. Slice the duck breasts lengthwise and as thinly as possible and fan out the meat in the center of each plate. Arrange the thighs and drumsticks on either side of the duck breasts and serve at once.

My sauces are stock reductions enriched with butter. I know of no other way to achieve equal purity and concentration of flavor. This is a higher level of sauce making and it requires a lot of time and energy to boil down the various ingredients. I think this is the direction sauces have been pointing to over the last thirty years…We go through forty quarts of stock a day at Panache and the dining room seats forty. That's what I mean by reduction cooking.

PANACHE

DUCK STOCK

carcasses, necks and giblets,
  from the 2 previous ducks
1 large onion, quartered
2 large carrots,
  coarsely chopped
2 ribs celery, chopped

2 cloves garlic, buised
2 tablespoons tomato paste
  bouquet garni of bay leaf,
  thyme and parsley
20 black peppercorns
2 quarts cold water

1. Roast the duck carcasses in a hot oven until thoroughly browned.
   When the bones begin to brown, add onion, carrots and celery and
   brown them as well.
2. Transfer the duck bones and vegetables to a large stockpot, discarding fat. Add the remaining ingredients. Bring the stock to a boil,
   skim and reduce heat to a simmer.
3. Simmer 3 to 5 hours, skimming from time to time to remove surface
   scum, adding cold water as necessary to end up with 7 cups of stock.
4. Strain and thoroughly degrease before using.

*Like most people who have opened restaurants, I tried a number of times and
failed before I opened Panache. The first try, you get so far before you run
into an obstacle you can't surmount. As you persist, the obstacles get fewer
and fewer. It took me ten years, but I finally made it.*

*A good cook is a good cook. Either you are or you aren't. I think I have a
talent for it. There is something special about me that comes out when I am
cooking.*

GREEN BEANS WITH GARLIC

1 pound green beans,
    washed and snapped
¼ cup unsalted butter

1 clove garlic,
    peeled and bruised
   salt and pepper

1. Cook the beans in at least 4 quarts of salted, boiling water for 3 minutes or to taste. They should remain a little crunchy. Remove beans and immerse immediatley in ice-cold water. (This fixes the bright green color.)

2. Melt butter in a sauté pan and add the garlic and thoroughly drained green beans. Sauté to warm the beans and sprinkle with salt and pepper. Remove garlic and serve beans on a separate vegetable plate.

A woman once said, "I can't understand why Bruce Frankel is so successful. He doesn't even French his string beans!" It doesn't really matter if each little detail is perfect. I don't go around and measure each vegetable julienne with a micrometer. The taste of the food matters more than how the green beans are cut.

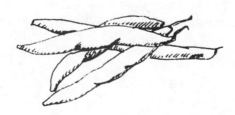

TANGERINE MOUSSE

juice of 2 tangerines, or
   enough to yield ½ cup
2 tablespoons fresh
   lemon juice
1½ teaspoons unflavored
   gelatin
3 eggs

¼ cup plus 2 tablespoons
   sugar
1 cup heavy cream
1½ teaspoons grated
   tangerine rind
pinch of salt
TANGERINE SHELLS

1. Pour the tangerine and lemon juices over the gelatin and leave for 15 minutes to soften.
2. Whisk the egg yolks with ¼ cup sugar for 5 minutes or until the mixture falls from the whisk or beater in a thick ribbon.
3. Set the yolk mixture over a pan of boiling water, reduce heat and stir constantly with a rubber spatula until the mixture becomes velvety and thickly coats the spatula.
4. Transfer the yolk mixture to a mixer and beat at a medium speed while warming the juice-gelatin mixture over boiling water. Add the juice-gelatin mixture to the yolk mixture, increasing mixer speed to fast. Beat until cool.
5. Beat the heavy cream with the grated tangerine rind to medium-stiff peaks. Fold into the cooled yolk mixture.
6. Beat the egg whites with a pinch of salt to medium-stiff peaks, beat in the remaining sugar and gently fold into mousse base. Chill 3 to 4 hours.
7. Just before serving, spoon the mousse generously into Tangerine Shells.

PANACHE

TANGERINE SHELLS

1 egg white
½ cup sugar
1½ tablespoons CLARIFIED
  BUTTER, melted
  (see index)

pinch of salt
1½ teaspoons grated
  tangerine rind
2½ tablespoons sifted flour

1. Combine the egg white, sugar, butter, salt and tangerine rind in a small mixing bowl.
2. Gradually whisk in the flour, beating until the mixture is free of lumps. Chill this batter for 1 hour.
3. Preheat the oven to 325° and butter and flour a large baking sheet.
4. Spoon the chilled batter onto the baking sheet in 6 drops, spreading each with the back of the spoon in a circular motion to form 6-inch rounds.
5. Bake the shells in preheated oven for 10 minutes or until golden brown. Carefully slide the shells offs the baking sheet with a metal spatula and press over overturned teacups to cool.

I believe that the dining experience should be free from distractions. There are no useless garnishes on the plates at Panache. The service is discreet. I've kept the décor as simple and understated as possible.

PARKER'S

Dinner for Four

Parker House Rolls

Warm Marinated Mussels

Méduillons de Veau Cressonnière

Heart of Palm Vinaigrette

Strawberries Romanoff

Wines:

With the Mussels—Pouilly–Fumé, St. Laurent, 1977

With the Veal—Meursault, Jaboulet Vercherre

With the Dessert—Dom Pérignon

Joseph Ribas, Chef

In 1825 a young man set out from Paris, Maine, with the clothes on his back and less than a dollar in his pocket to find his fortune in Boston. Thirty years later, he built a gleaming marble edifice on the corner of Tremont and School Streets, destined to become the premier hotel in New England. Harvey Parker rose from stable boy to restaurateur to millionaire. His hotel and dining establishment, the Parker House, has remained synonymous with high class and hospitality for 128 years.

"To dine here is to live," pronounced one enthusiast when Parker's restaurant opened in 1854. In an age when competent cooks earned eight dollars a week, Mr. Parker paid his chef, a Frenchman by the name of Sanzian, a staggering $5,000 a year for his culinary talents. During Sanzian's reign, many Parker House classics first appeared on the menu—Parker's Tripes, Boston Scrod (supposedly named for Mr. Scrod, one of the hotel's early managers), Boston Cream Pie,—but it was a German baker named Ward who made Parker's a household word with the invention of the moist Parker House Rolls. Dozens of nineteenth-century notables, including Dickens, Thackery, Emerson, Hawthorne, Longfellow and Sara Bernhardt, frequented the Parker House. The prestigious *Atlantic Monthly* was launched from one of Parker's private dining rooms in 1857.

The Parker House Hotel was completey rebuilt on its present site in 1925. Fifty years later, Parker's dining room received a million-dollar facelift. The sweeping hall seats 140 today and tie and jacket are de rigueur. Parker's bill of fare retains the flavor of the past in the time-honored Continental and New England specialties which appear on the menu. But Parker's also keeps apace with the '80s with its nouvelle cuisine offerings and stylish Sunday brunch.

"You've got to dedicate your whole life to this business," says executive chef Josef Ribas, who works ninety hours a week in the kitchen. Born in Guarda, Portugal, Ribas has worked all over Europe and Latin America and brings an international flair to his cuisine at the Parker House. Ribas came to Parker's in 1970; today he commands a kitchen brigade of forty. He delights in the richness of New England's sea fare and in the challenge of uniting Parker's past and future in his cuisine.

Tremont and School Streets
227-8600

PARKER HOUSE ROLLS

1 cup scalded milk
1 teaspoon salt
1 tablespoon sugar
5 tablespoons melted butter

½ cake yeast dissolved
in 2 tablespoons
lukewarm water
2½-3 cups bread flour

1. Place the milk, salt, sugar and 2 tablespoons melted butter into a bowl and mix well. Leave to cool slightly.
2. When the mixture is lukewarm, add the yeast and stir in enough flour to obtain a thickish dough which you can knead. Knead well, then leave the dough to rise 1 hour or until doubled in bulk.
3. Punch dough down and knead for 1 minute.
4. Shape the dough into 1-inch balls and place on a buttered baking sheet and cover. When the balls have risen to double in bulk, press down in the center with the floured handle of a wooden spoon.
5. Preheat oven to 375°.
6. Bake for 12 to 15 minutes.
7. Brush the tops of the rolls with more melted butter after baking and serve warm.

These rolls are the most famous dish on our menu. They were invented by a German baker named Ward in the middle of the last century. There was once a time when we would ship Parker House Rolls daily to New York and even as far as Philadelphia.

A chef must have creativity, otherwise he will not succeed. You cannot be an eight-hour chef. I work fourteen to sixteen hours a day, six days a week. There are times when I go five weeks straight without a day off.

WARM MARINATED MUSSELS

32 mussels	¾ cup dry white wine
2 tablespoons finely minced shallots	¾ cup *FISH VELOUTÉ*
1 clove garlic, minced	½ cup whipping cream
1 tablespoon whole black peppercorns	juice of ½ lemon
3 tablespoons butter	dash of Worcestershire sauce
	salt and pepper

1. Thoroughly scrub the mussels under running water and remove threads, discarding any mussels which fail to close when tapped.
2. Lightly sauté the shallots, garlic, and peppercorns in the butter. Add the mussels, wine, and Fish Velouté. Simmer until the mussels open. Transfer the mussels to a platter and keep warm.
3. Add the cream and simmer the sauce for 5 minutes or until slightly reduced and thickened.
4. Add the lemon juice, Worcestershire sauce, and salt and pepper to taste. Strain the sauce over the mussels and serve immediately.

The best mussels are the ones you pick right off the rocks among the seaweed. I would not suggest using the cultivated mussels—they don't have as much flavor . . . To get rid of the sand, soak the mussels in a gallon of cold, salted water with a handful of corn meal for a day. The mussels eat the corn meal and spit out the sand.

You have to have a feeling for the clientele. There are certain dishes which I would like to do, but the public just won't buy them. It's important to work closely with the maître d', to find out what people like.

FISH VELOUTÉ

6 tablespoons butter
6 tablespoons flour

4 cups FISH STOCK
salt and pepper
lemon juice

1. Melt the butter in a saucepan and whisk in the flour. Cook this mixture for 3 minutes, but do not let brown.
2. Add Fish Stock, whisking steadily.
3. Simmer for 30 minutes, correcting the seasoning with salt, pepper, and lemon juice before using.

Note: It is not practical to make Fish Velouté in quantities less than 4 cups. The excess sauce here makes a delicious accompaniment for any seafood dish and can be frozen.

FISH STOCK

1 pound white fish bones,
    thoroughly rinsed
1 small onion

1 rib celery
1 tablespoon chopped shallots
1 teaspoon black peppercorns
1 cup dry white wine

1. Place the fish bones, onion, celery, shallots, peppercorns, wine, and 3 cups water in a saucepan and gradually bring to boil.
2. Skim the stock, reduce heat and gently simmer for 30 minutes.
3. Strain before using.

MÉDAILLONS DE VEAU CRESSONNIÉRRE
Veal Medallions with Watercress Sauce

1¼ cups unsalted butter,
  at room temperature
8 (3-ounce) veal medallions,
  cut from the loin or
  tenderloin
1 carrot, diced
1 small onion, diced
2 ribs celery, diced

1 tablespoon minced shallots
1 teaspoon black peppercorns
1 cup dry white wine
1 large bunch watercress,
  leaves and stems separated
2 cups whipping cream
  salt and pepper
  lemon juice

1. Melt ¼ cup of the butter and gently sauté the veal medallions 4 to 5 minutes per side. Do not brown. When the medallions are cooked, or nearly cooked, transfer to a platter and keep warm.
2. Place the carrot, onion, celery, shallots, peppercorns, wine, and watercress stems in the pan and simmer until the wine is reduced to about ¼ cup. Add the cream and continue simmering until ½ cup liquid remains.
3. Working off direct heat, but over a warm spot on the stove, gradually whisk in the remaining 1 cup butter to make a thick, silky sauce. This should take about 5 minutes. You can warm the sauce over a low heat, but if it boils, it will separate.
4. Strain the sauce and correct the seasoning with salt, pepper, and lemon juice.
5. Add the watercress leaves to the hot sauce and spoon over the veal medallions. Serve at once.

When you go to buy veal, look at the color. The whiter the meat, the better the veal. Good veal should be tender, not stringy. The best veal is milk-fed veal—once the calf starts to eat grass, the color of the meat darkens. It becomes tough and you want to avoid it . . I slightly undercook my veal—I have always done that. The veal should never get browned when you cook it. To keep your veal nice and white, never overheat your frying pan.

People are getting away from the rich French sauces. Roux are out—the new sauces are made with wine or stock reductions—just like your mother used to do it at home. We were one of the first Boston restaurants to put nouvelle cuisine selections on our menu—they've been extremely popular.

HEARTS OF PALM VINAIGRETTE

1 large can hearts of palm	¼ cup chopped parsley
1 head Boston lettuce	4 lemon wedges
1 tomato, sliced in wedges	VINAIGRETTE SAUCE
4 thin slices red onion	

1. Quarter the larger hearts of palm lengthwise, leaving the smaller ones whole, and arrange over the lettuce on four chilled salad plates. Garnish with the tomato, onion, parsley, and lemon wedges.
2. Pour Vinaigrette Sauce over the hearts of palm 5 minutes before serving.

VINAIGRETTE SAUCE

1 teaspoon freshly chopped red onion	¼ cup olive oil
1 red pimiento	1 tablespoon red wine vinegar
1 teaspoon chopped fresh tarragon	dash of Worcestershire sauce
1 teaspoon chopped parsley	salt and white pepper
1 tablespoon lemon juice	

Purée all ingredients in a blender.

STRAWBERRIES ROMANOFF

¾ cup whipping cream
2 pints strawberries,
   washed and hulled

½ cup orange liqueur
   (Grand Marnier)
2 tablespoons confectioner's
   sugar

1. Whip the cream until it forms soft peaks.
2. Fold the strawberries into the cream.
3. Sprinkle the orange liqueur and confectioners' sugar over the strawberry/cream mixture and serve in saucer-shaped champagne glasses.

Cooking today is not like in the old days. When I took my apprenticeship in Portugal, if I did something wrong, my chef would slap me across the face. He would make me wash pots for four days straight, without doing anything else. Thank goodness those days are passed. Today a chef has to be a teacher and a counselor.

RESTAURANT GENJI

Dinner for Six

Hamaguri-Siru
(Clam Soup)

Kaibashira-Sumiso
(Uncooked Marinated Scallops)

Tempura
(Batter-Fried Vegetables)

Sukiyaki
(Japanese Pan-Cooked Beef)

Ginger Ice Cream

Wine:

As an Apértif—Plum Wine

With the Meal—Saki

Toshio Matsumoto, Owner
Shinji Muraki, Chef

To cognoscenti of the Orient, the Genji were a royal family of twelfth-century Kyoto. To connoisseurs of Eastern cooking, Genji is a chic Japanese restaurant on Newberry Street. "I have tried to recreate the atmosphere of an imperial Japanese palace at my restaurant, says Genji owner Toshio Matsumoto. The costly misu screens and coffered ceilings, the elaborately carved Shinto shrine and the kimonoed waitresses lend the Restaurant Genji an air of royal majesty.

The Genji, which opened in 1975, offers two very different dining experiences. The downstairs specializes in kappo—Japan's classical cuisine—served in stunning Bento lacquerware. The upstairs features teppan—Japanese steakhouse dining—with swashbuckling chefs who cook right on the tables. Aficionados of vinegared rice and raw fish cakes line up at Genji's sushi bar for impeccably fresh sushi and sashimi. For the cross-legged crowd there's an authentic Japanese tearoom, with grass mats and a life-size tiger mural. Tokyo-born Toshio Matsumoto brings extensive food experience to his restaurant. The son of a great Japanese restaurant family (his brother owns thirty restaurants in Tokyo), Matsumoto had several restaurants in New York prior to opening Genji. He sees himself as a culinary ambassador. "The Japanese consulate does not work very hard here, so I bring Oriental culture to the American people through the stomach," he says with a smile.

327 Newbury Street
267-5656

HAMAGURI-SIRU

12 cherrystone clams, thoroughly scrubbed	1 teaspoon salt
6 cups water	3 tablespoons dried bonito
1 tablespoon sake	6 paper-thin lemon slices
	6 sprigs watercress

1. Place clams and water in a saucepan and simmer until clams open. Transfer clams with shells to six soup bowls, 2 clams per bowl.

2. Add the sake, salt and dried bonito to the clam broth and simmer very gently for 5 minutes. Strain the broth through a cheesecloth into the soup bowls.

3. Garnish each bowl with a lemon slice and sprig of watercress for serving.

Note: Sake is Japanese rice wine. Dried bonito, called katsuobushi, is pre-flaked dried fish use for making fish stocks and flavoring sauces. Both are available in most Oriental markets. Commercial fish or clam base can be substituted for katsuobushi.

KAIBASHIRA-SUMISO

¼ cup sugar
½ cup rice vinegar
2 egg yolks
½ cup sake

2 teaspoons Dijon-style mustard
1 cup miso
18 medium-size sea scallops, cut in half

Combine sugar, vinegar, egg yolks, sake, mustard and miso and stir in the scallops. Marinate at least 3 hours prior to serving.

Note: Miso is a strong, salty paste made from fermented soybeans. It is used to flavor soups and sauces. For this dish you should use *shiro miso*, which is lighter in color than *aka miso*. Because of its high salt content, *miso* will keep up to a year unrefrigerated even when opened.

The West should eat more seafood and more vegetables, like the Japanese. Too much meat makes people wild, gives them body odor, makes them lose their hair. I suggest that the American people eat more seaweed; it will keep them from going bald.

Japanese soy sauce is superior because we use fermented rice to make it. It contains a certain kind of bacteria, like penicillin, which is good for the body. It has a nice taste too—slightly sweet.

TEMPURA

1 medium-size sweet potato, peeled and sliced into ¼" rounds

2 carrots, peeled and cut into ¼" strips

12 small asparagus stalks or 12 string beans, snapped

1 green pepper, seeded and cut into ¼" strips

12 large shrimp, shelled and deveined

3 eggs

1 cup flour

½ teaspoon baking powder

1 cup ice-cold water

DIPPING SAUCE

1. Cut vegetables and arrange by kind with shrimp on a platter.
2. Beat the eggs in a bowl and sift in the flour and baking powder. Whisk the mixture, adding enough water to obtain a thin batter about the consistencey of heavy cream.
3. Heat at least 2 inches of oil to 375° in a wide deep-frying pan or electric skillet. Using chopsticks or a fork, dip one piece of food at a time into the tempura batter and drop it into the oil. Fry ingredients of the same kind together, but do not overcrowd the pan.
4. Place tempura on paper towels to drain and serve at once with Dipping Sauce.

DIPPING SAUCE

2 teapoons dried bonito

¼ cup boiling water

¼ cup mirin

¼ cup Japanese soy sauce

1. Add the bonito to boiling water and very gently simmer for 5 minutes.
2. Add mirin and soy sauce and strain. Sauce can be made ahead of time and should be served in small ramekins or little ceramic saucers.

Note: Mirin is sweet rice wine, sold in many Oriental grocery stores. While cream sherry is quite different, it makes a passible substitute. The Dipping Sauce can be made with fish or chicken stock instead of bonita and water, but the flavor, though tasty, will not be authentic.

SUKIYAKI

1½-2 pounds beef sirloin,
         shaved into ⅛" slices
   1 can agar-agar noodles
   2 onions, very thinly sliced
   1 bunch watercress, thick
         stems removed
  12 ounces fresh spinach,
         washed and stems removed

   1 (12-ounce) package
         mushrooms, washed and
         thinly sliced
  ¼ cup soy sauce
   2 tablespoons sugar
   2 tablespoons sake
   2 tablespoons mirin
   2 tablespoons water

1. Heat a large skillet or large electric frying pan and add beef fat (2 to 3 cubes). Push the cubes around with chopsticks to thoroughly coat the pan with melted fat and then remove.
2. Arrange the meat, noodles and vegetables on a platter.
3. Combine soy sauce, sugar, sake, mirin and water.
4. Add half the meat, noodles and vegetables to the hot pan, keeping each ingredient separate. Fry each until tender, but do not overcook the vegetables.
5. Pour half the sauce over the sukiyaki and wait until it begins to sizzle.
6. Serve at once. Cook the remaining ingredients the same way.

Note: Agar-agar noodles are made from gelatin-rich seaweed. They are available canned in most Oriental grocery stores.

Sukiyaki is usually prepared right at the table in Japan. The tables in Genji's teppan rooms have special heated surfaces for cooking sukiyaki and teriyaki in front of our guests. You can use an electric frying pan or hot plate and skillet when preparing sukiyaki at the table at home.

GINGER ICE CREAM

1½ pints homemade
          vanilla ice cream

6 tablespoons coarsely
        chopped candied ginger

1. Soften the ice cream with a wooden spoon and stir in the ginger to taste.
2. Return to the freezer to harden for a least 2 hours prior to serving.

Dinner for Six

Hot Lobster Sausage with Vegetable Slaw

Duckling with Ginger and Scallions

Lemon Mousseline

Wines:

Robert Mondavi Fumé Blanc Reserve 1980

Pine Ridge (Oak Knoll District) Gewürztraminer 1981

Clos du Bois Late Harvest Johannisberg Riesling 1981

Lydia Shire, Executive Chef

Bradford Cole, Sous Chef

Kilian Weigand, Pastry Chef

Robert Cioffe, Maitre d'

When *Food and Wine Magazine* named Jasper White and Lydia Shire in its roster of the "100 Best Chefs in North America," recently, Bostonians were not surprised. For the past 6 years, the two have worked together at many of the top restaurants in town, including the Cafe Plaza and Parker's at the venerable Parker House. When the Bostonian Hotel opened across from Quinsy Market in the fall of 1982, its owner wisely chose White and Shire to head the kitchens of its elegant restaurant, Seasons. Their efforts have drawn rave reviews from the *Globe,* the *Boston Herald,* and *Boston Magazine,* making Seasons one hotel restaurant where the locals outnumber the tourists.

Located on the 4th floor of the hotel, Seasons offers a fine view of the historic Faneuil Hall Market area through its arched, windowed walls and ceilings. In a more contemporary vein, a push of a button electronically raises and lowers the marble-patterned curtain to shield guests from unwanted sunlight. The dining room seats 150 in comfortable Louis XV chairs at well-spaced tables. The waiters wear black tie, but their service manages to be friendly as well as professional.

Lydia Shire is now in sole command of the kitchen and Seasons' menus, which she changes four times per year to feature appropriate seasonal foods. Following the grass roots movement sweeping American restaurants, Shire applies contemporary European cooking techniques to indiginous New England ingredients. The desserts of Culinary Institute of America-trained pastry chef Kilian Weigand, however, are Continental in their luscious excess. Unique to Boston is the Season's wine list, featuring exclusively American vintages. The final touch: the coffees, including whole bean decaffinated, are freshly ground before brewing.

Corner of North Street and Blackstone Street

HOT LOBSTER SAUSAGE WITH VEGETABLE SLAW

3-4 feet of pork casing
2 cups papaya juice
2 (3-pound) live lobsters
1 egg white
2 red peppers, roasted,
    peeled and seeded
2 sticks (½ pound) unsalted
    butter, room temperature
½ cup fresh bread crumbs
1 carrot, peeled and
    very finely chopped

1 stalk celery, finely chopped
2 cloves garlic, minced
2 tablespoons each fresh chop-
    ped parsley and chervil
    fresh black pepper
    cayenne pepper
1 cup CLARIFIED BUTTER
    for serving (see index)
    VEGETABLE SLAW

1. Thoroughly rinse the sausage casing and soak it for 24 hours in papaya juice. (This helps tenderize the casing.) Rinse again.

2. Kill one lobster using either of the two methods described below. Remove the raw meat from the tail section and reserve. Cut it in half lengthwise and remove the black vein.

3. Cook the remainder of this lobster with the whole one in rapidly boiling water for 10 minutes. When the lobsters are cool enough to handle, remove the meat from the tail, claws, bodies, and small legs, and cut it into a ½-inch dice. Reserve.

4. Prepare the forcemeat: Puree the uncooked lobster tail in a food processor with the egg white, peppers, 1 stick butter, and the bread crumbs. Reserve in a cool place.

5. Melt the remaining butter in a small pan and "sweat" the carrot, celery and garlic; that is cook them, covered, over a low heat until soft. Gently mix the vegetables and diced lobster meat into the lobster forcemeat, seasoning with the herbs and pepper. Salt should not be necessary.

6. Stuff the sausages: Knot one end of the casing and pull the other end onto your sausage stuffer. (Note; do not use a stuffer with a meat grinder, as the blade will chop the lobster mixture too finely.) Loosely fill the casing, twisting the sausage in opposite directions every 3 inches to make links. If you do not have a sausage stuffer, pull the casing over the metal tip of a piping bag, and load the bag with lobster mixture. Keeping the casing in place with one hand, squeeze the stuffing from the bag with the other. The sausages can be prepared up to 48 hours ahead of time and stored in the refrigerator.

7. To cook the lobster sausages, prick them lightly with a needle, and place them in gently simmering water for 4-5 minutes, or until firm. (Note: do not overcook.) Alternately, the sausages can be steamed. Serve the sausages on warm salad plates with melted butter and Vegetable Slaw.

To execute this recipe, you must use raw lobster meat. The easiest way to extract the meat is to kill the lobster by plunging a large knife lengthwise through the head directly in back of the eyes. (The lobster dies instantly, although the body may continue to jerk for several seconds.) If you are unable, or unwilling to kill the lobsters in this fashion, boil it for 3-4 minutes, and then extract the meat.

Pork casing is available packed in salt at most supermarkets and quality butcher shops. The casings will keep almost indefinitely in salt. When you are ready to use them, simply cut off the desired length and wash it thoroughly outside and in with cold water. To tenderize the casings, soak them in papaya juice, which contains a powerful enzyme used in many commercial meat tenderizers.

To roast red peppers, place the peppers directly on the burner over a high flame, or, if you have electric heat, under the broiler. Char the peppers on all sides: the skin should be completely black. Wrap the peppers in wet paper towels for 10 minutes (this helps "steam" off the skin). Using your fingers or a paring knife, scrape off the charred skin under cold running water. To seed the peppers, cut out the stem end and remove the core.

VEGETABLE SLAW

1 small head green cabbage	1 small green pepper
1 carrot, peeled	3 tablespoons unsalted butter
1 zucchini, split and cored	½ teaspoon caraway seed
1 branch celery	salt and freshly ground
1 small red onion	black pepper

Thinly slice the cabbage and blanch it in rapidly boiling water for 30 seconds. Drain. Chop the remaining vegetables as finely as possible, or cut them into thin slivers. Melt the butter in a sauté pan, and cook the cabbage and vegetables with the seasonings until crispy tender. Serve warm.

DUCKLING WITH GINGER AND SCALLIONS

3 (5 pound) fresh ducks	oil for frying pan
1 (3 ounce) ginger root	6 scallion pancakes (available
½ head garlic	at Chinese markets)
1½ cups soy sauce	6 scallions, thinly sliced
¾ cup sherry	steamed shiitake (black)
3 tablespoons honey	mushrooms or other wild
¼ cup sesame oil	mushrooms

1. Preheat oven to 325°.
2. Prepare the duck or have your butcher do it. Remove the legs from the carcass and flatten them slightly with a heavy cleaver. Place the duck back side down and remove the breasts. Make a lengthwise incision along the right side of the breast bone, and keeping the knife next to the ribs, cutting around the wing, remove the right breast in a single piece. Trim off all shiny sinew and excess fat. Remove the left breast the same way. Reserve the carcass.
3. Finely chop the ginger and garlic and combine with the soy sauce, sherry, honey, and sesame oil. Marinate the duck legs in this mixture for 2 hours.

4. Place the duck carcasses in a roasting pan and arrange the legs on top. Roast the legs for 2¼ hours. Marinate the duck breasts in the soy mixture while the legs are roasting (but for no longer than 2 hours).

5. A few minutes before serving, heat a lightly oiled frying pan over a medium flame and add the duck breasts, skin side down. Sauté the breasts for 4 minutes or until the skin is almost black. The skin should be very crispy; the breast meat, medium-rare. Leave the breasts stand for 5 minutes.

6. Meanwhile, slit the thigh of the duck legs and remove the bone. Warm the legs, skin side down, in a frying pan until the skin is crisp.

7. To serve, place a scallion pancake on each of six warm plates. Set the duck leg on top. Slice the breast lengthwise into four or five slices, and fan them out around the leg. Sprinkle the duck with a little marinade and sprinkle the plate with scallions. Serve the steamed black mushrooms on the side.

This recipe shows how Seasons chef Lydia Shire borrows freely from cuisines of the Far East as well as those of North America and the Continent. The soy marinade helps assure a crisp duck skin. Scallion pancakes can be found at any grocery store or bakery in Chinatown.

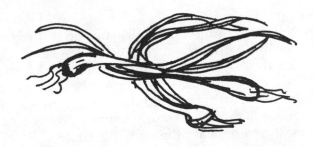

LEMON MOUSSELINE

½ ounce (2 envelopes)
  gelatin
  juice of 5 large lemons
  grated rind of 3 lemons
6 eggs, separated

1 cup sugar
1½ cups heavy cream
2 pints fresh raspberries
1 10" sponge cake

1. Soften the gelatin in the lemon juice in a small bowl. Set the bowl in a shallow pan of simmering water, and heat the gelatin until it melts. Stir in the lemon rind.

2. Beat the egg yolks, and ⅓ cup of sugar together in a non-aluminum bowl for 5 minutes, or until the mixture falls from the whisk or beater in a thick yellow ribbon.

3. Whip the cream to soft peaks.

4. Beat the egg whites to stiff peaks, sprinkling in the remaining sugar as the whites begin to stiffen.

5. Fold the gelatin mixture into the ribboned yolks. Fold the yolk mixture into the stiffly beaten whites. Fold the cream into the egg mixture, with the raspberries.

6. Line the bottom of a 10-inch spring-form pan with a thin slice of sponge cake, and spoon in the mousseline mixture. Refrigerate for at least 4-5 hours, or until firm.

7. To serve, unmold the mousseline and cut it into twelve slices. Decorate with more raspberries and whipped cream, if desired. (The mousseline can also be served frozen.) Serves 12.

This recipe is a culinary play on appearances. It is a mousse that looks like a cake when served. The garnish of sponge cake and fresh raspberries is optional.

Upstairs at the Pudding

Dinner for Six

Prosciutto with Figs and Melons

Cappelletti with Fresh Ricotta and Snails

Muscovy Duck with Red Wine

Asparagus with Crème Fraiche

Espresso Granita

Wines:

Asti Spumante (Bonardi)

Vernoccia di San Geminiano 1982 (Ricardo Falchini)

Taurasi 1973 (Mastroberardino)

Grappa with Dessert

Mary-Catherine Deibel, Proprietor
Michael Silver, Proprietor and Chef

Upstairs at the Pudding is, admittedly, a peculiar name for a restaurant, nor does the word "pudding" begin to hint at the glories of Northern Italian gastronomy featured on the nightly-changing menu. Rather, Pudding refers to Harvard's historic Hasty Pudding Club on Holyoke Street, on the top floor of which chef Michael Silver and Mary-Catherine Deibel opened this fashionable restaurant in 1981. The restaurant's first guest was Ella Fitzgerald, who recieved the Hasty Pudding Club "Woman of the Year" award at a special banquet here the week the restaurant opened. The critics soon followed, proclaiming Upstairs at the Pudding the forerunner of the Northern Italian Culinary revolution sweeping Boston.

The Pudding dining room, appointed with forest green walls and cantilevered ceiling timbers, boasts the contemporary elegance of tables draped with pink cloths and set with shining brass service plates and fresh cut flowers. The walls are decorated with playbills, many of them antiques, from past Hasty Pudding theatrics. On nights of performances, the music drifts up to the dining room from the theater below.

It is no accident that the food, service, and very setting of Upstairs at the Pudding should seem so theatrical. For many years Pudding co-proprietor Mary-Catherine Deibel was a classical music concert manager, and from 1971 to 1982 she helped to initiate and manage the music program at the popular Cambridge cabaret/restaurant, the Peasant Stock. Pudding chef Michael Silver, a Phi Beta Kappa gradate of the University of Illinois, also worked at the Peasant Stock, prior to traveling to Italy in the summer of 1977 to study classical Northern Italian cooking with Marcella Hazan. Upstairs at the Pudding house specialties include the *cappelletti* with snails and the muscovy duck dish featured in the following recipes.

10 Holyoke Street, Cambridge

PROSCIUTTO WITH FIGS AND MELON

12 fresh kadota figs
1 tablespoon finely chopped
    fresh thyme leaves
¼ cup honey

½ cup warm water
12 very thin slices of
    prosciutto ham
1 ripe melon of any kind

1. Take six of the figs and slice them into six even wedges. (Reserve the remainder.) Dust the wedges lightly with thyme. Thin the honey with the water and dip the prosciutto slices in it. Cut the prosciutto into ¼-inch strips and use them to wrap up the thyme-coated fig slices. Cut the melon into thin slices.

2. Just before serving, cut the remaining figs into six wedges and arrange them on chilled salad plates with the ham-wrapped figs and melon slices.

Kadota figs have purple skins with a delicate white flesh inside. If good melon is unavailable, feel free to substitute fresh berries or other fruits.

CAPPELLETTI WITH FRESH RICOTTA AND SNAILS

24	Burgundian snails (available canned in gourmet shops	1	pint fresh ricotta cheese
		2	cups semolina flour
1½	sticks(12 tablespoons) unsalted butter	6	large eggs
		2	teaspoons milk
4	cloves garlic, peeled		salt
½	cup fresh chopped Italian (flat leaf) parsley	½	cup freshly grated Parmesan cheese
		¼	cup heavy cream

1. To prepare the filling, soak the snails in cold water for 30 minutes to remove the sulphur taste, then drain. Melt the butter in a sauté pan over low heat with the garlic cloves. Cook the garlic until it becomes translucent, then discard and add the snails. Cook the snails in the garlic butter over low heat turning from time to time, for 5 minutes.

2. Remove one-quarter of the garlic butter from the pan and reserve it for the sauce. Increase heat to high. When the butter hisses, remove the pan from the heat and stir in ¼ cup chopped parsley. Fold in the ricotta cheese, so that it melts and coats the snails. Refrigerate the filling for at least 2 hours (it can be made the day before), or until the cheese and butter gel.

3. Meanwhile, mound the flour on a large, clean, flat work surface. Using the bottom of a tea cup, make a "well" in the center of the flour. Crack the eggs into the well with the milk, and, using a fork to beat the eggs, gradually incorporate the flour until the egg mixture is no longer runny. Knead the dough with the heel of your palm for 5 minutes or until smooth. You may need to add a little more flour. When the dough is the right consistancy, your thumb print should remain visible when pressed into the dough. Note: the pasta dough can be prepared up to 48 hours ahead of time and stored tightly wrapped in the refrigerator. Once the dough is rolled (see next step), you must proceed very quickly.

4. Using a pasta machine, roll the dough into sheets as thin as possible. (Rolled pasta dough dries out very quickly, so work fast, and cover the sheets with a cotton dish towel until ready to use.) Cut the pasta sheets into 2-inch squares, and place a ricotta and butter-coated snail in the center of each. To shape the *cappelletti,* fold one corner of the square over the snail to meet the opposite corner and press the edges to seal in the snail. You should wind up with a triangular shaped dumpling. Place the triangle on the back of your index finger, with the apex pointing up. Fold the bottom corners of the triangle around your finger and pinch them together to seal in front. (The dumpling should now be shaped like a ring or a bishop's mitre.) Slip the *capelletti* off your finger and place on a baking sheet lined with a clean cotton dish towel. Refrigerate the *capelletti* for 30 minutes. Invert each so that the air dries the underside, and refrigerate for 30 minutes more. Note: the *cappelletti* will keep in the refrigerator for 4-5 hours. If you do not cook them right away, however, add an extra minute to the cooking time.

5. To cook and serve the *cappelletti,* bring at least 5 quarts water to a rapid boil and add ½ teaspoon salt. Add the dumplings and cook for 8 minutes, or until the thickest part of each dumpling (the sealed part) is *al dente.*

6. Drain the *cappelletti* and toss them with the reserved garlic butter in a large sauté pan over medium heat. Sprinkle in the Parmesan cheese, followed by the cream. When the cheese melts, stir in the remaining parsley and serve at once, figuring four *cappelletti* per person.

Semolina flour is made from durham wheat from North Dakota. It contains more gluten than regular wheat and produces a nice, firm pasta. Under-salt the recipe along the way, as the Parmesan cheese added at the end is salty. Note that the salt is added to the pasta water after it boils; presalting the water gives the pasta a stale taste.

MUSCOVY DUCK WITH RED WINE

6 Muscovy duck breasts, boned, and skinned	2-3 teaspoons CLARIFIED BUTTER (see index)
24 fresh sage leaves	½ cup balsamic vinegar
6 prosciutto or Westphalian ham slices	3 cups dry red wine
2 eggs	salt and fresh black pepper
	FRIED SAGE LEAVES
	CANDIED SHALLOTS

1. Trim the duck breasts of all shiny sinew. Butterfly each breast: lay it flat on a cutting board, cut it almost in half lengthwise, leaving the far edge attached. Open the butterflied breast like a book, and spread it on a sheet of waxed paper. Place four sage leaves on top of the breast and cover with a slice of prosciutto. Place another sheet of waxed paper on top, and using a scaloppine pounder or the flat side of a cleaver, flatten the breast to the thickness of a veal scaloppinni. Note: it is best to pound the duck with glancing blows—the idea here is to stretch the meat not crush it.

2. Beat the eggs with 1 teaspoon water until very smooth. Heat the butter in a large sauté pan over high heat. When the butter just begins to smoke, dip each flattened duck breast in egg batter and place it, ham side down, in the pan. Sauté the duck for 2 minutes, or until the first appearance of juices on the top; then turn the breasts and sauté for half the time needed for the first side. Remove the duck scaloppine. from the pan and keep warm.

3. Prepare the sauce: Add the vinegar and wine to the pan, and boil rapidly over high heat until the original volume of the liquid is reduced by two-thirds. Season lightly with salt and pepper. Place the duck breasts on warmed dinner plates, and over each spoon 2-3 tablespoons of sauce. Garnish the duck with the vegetables below and serve at once.

FRIED SAGE LEAVES

1 cup CLARIFIED
    BUTTER (see index)

1 bunch fresh sage leaves,
    stems tied together
    with a rubber band

1. Heat ¼-inch Clarified Butter over a high flame in a small sauté pan. When the butter "quivers" and is on the verge of smoking, holding the sage by the stems, plunge the leaves into the pan. The leaves should fan out. Fry the sage for 1-2 minutes, or until the leaves are crisp and dark green. Transfer the sage to paper towels to drain, and cut off the stems. The leaves will remain crisp if kept warm, and can be reheated in a low oven.

CANDIED SHALLOTS

24 large shallots
 2 tablespoons melted butter
 ⅓ cup red wine vinegar

2 tablespoons dry red wine
3 tablespoons sugar

Cut the ends off and peel the shallots. Fit them tightly into a low-sided, heavy-bottomed pan. Add the remaining ingredients, and stir to thoroughly coat the shallots. Braise the shallots over a very low heat, uncovered, for 4 hours, or until the shallots are soft and shiny, and the liquid has completely evaporated.

If all the liquid evaporates before the shallots are cooked, add a little water. If the shallots become soft before the wine and vinegar evaporate, pour off the liquid, add 1 tablespoon butter and 1 tablespoon sugar, and cook the shallots over a medium heat, until they are coated with a syrupy glaze. Try to disturb the shallots as little as possible, so as to keep them whole.

ASPARAGUS SALAD WITH CRÈME FRAÎCHE

30 jumbo asparagus stalks
      salt
 3 tablespoons apricot
      kernel oil
	½ cup crèmefraîche
	     or sour cream
	 6 drained sun-dried tomatoes,
	     cut into thin slivers

1. Snap the woody ends off the asparagus, and peel and trim each stalk. Cook the asparagus in rapidly boiling, salted water to cover for no more than 1 minute. Drain the asparagus and plunge into ice water (this fixes the bright green color and prevents overcooking). When cool, drain the spears, and blot dry with paper towels. The asparagus can be prepared ahead to this stage and refrigerated until serving.

2. To serve, roll each asparagus spear in apricot kernel oil—it should be *very lightly* coated. Arrange the spears in a fan pattern on chilled salad plates, five to a plate. Spoon a dollop of *crème fraîche* at the apex of each fan, and sprinkle the asparagus with the slivered tomato.

Note: To make *crème fraîche*, combine two parts heavy cream with one part sour cream. Heat to 85°—no higher. Let the mixture stand overnight in a *loosely* covered glass jar. It should taste sourish and be quite thick. *Crème fraîche* will keep for 5-8 days in the refrigerator.

Choose plump stalks for this refreshing asparagus salad. Apricot kernel oil is available in health food stores (substitute any vegetable oil if you cannot find it). Crème fraîche is French heavy cream, which is thick and slightly fermented; sour cream makes an acceptable substitute. A specialty of Ligura (the Italian Riviera), sun-dried tomatoes are tomatoes which have been dried on the vine and marinated in olive oil.

ESPRESSO GRANITA

1 pound espresso coffee,
 freshly and finely ground
1 quart boiling water

1-1½ cups superfine sugar
1 cup heavy cream,
 stiffly whipped

1. Place half the coffee in a Melior-type coffee pot with half the water, and brew for 10 minutes. (To make the coffee, simply push down the plunger.) Repeat with the remaining coffee. The final brew should be very strong.
2. Mix in sugar until the coffee tastes a little too sweet. (It will taste just right when frozen.)
3. Freeze the coffee mixture in you ice cream churn, following the directions of the manufacturer, until it is firm and grainy. Serve the granita in champagne glasses with a swirl of unsweetened whipped cream.

A granita is a grainy Italian sherbet. We prefer the richness of coffee brewed in a Melior-type pot. The exact amount of sweetening is left to your taste. This recipe serves 12.

The Voyagers

Dinner for Six

Turban of Salmon, Sole and Spinach

Chicken Aficionado

Honey-Lemon Carrots

Green and Gold Squash

Strawberries Cassis

Wines:

With the Fish—Charles Heidsiek Brut Champagne 1973

With the Chicken—Château Brane-Cantenac 1966

*With the Dessert—Piesporter Goldtröpfchen Riesling
Auslese 1976*

Dorothy Koval, Chef

The Voyagers restaurant near Harvard Square may be the only eating establishment in Boston where quests can dine under the stars in a rooftop greenhouse surrounded by lush foliage and murmuring fountains. Then again, few restaurants pamper their clients with calligraphic place cards, hand-blown stemware and nightly concerts of live harp and harpsichord music. It is rare in this day to find a restaurant which attends to such a multitude of details. At the Voyagers, guests are continually reminded how much the setting, ambiance, music, tableware and service of a restaurant enhance the cuisine. The three dining rooms at the Voyagers feature revolving exhibits of contemporary and Oriental art, plus prints of the Old Masters. A handsome newsletter keeps patron abreast of the latest expositions. It is no accident that the visual arts and music figure prominently in the dining experience at the Voyagers. Chef Dorothy Koval gave up a career as an art gallery director in 1977 to take charge of the Voyagers kitchen.

"I had never had any restaurant experience before the Voyagers," recalls Chef Koval with a smile. "The freedom from the prejudices of the professional, however, has proved much more a benefit than a handicap." Koval describes here cooking as a personal cuisine which changes seasonally. She leans toward the specialties of France and Italy to a point and then her imagination takes over.

The entire staff at the Voyagers sees cooking as a total experience which begins in the garden and ends in the dining room. The cooks grow their own herbs, make their own vinegar, smoke their own quail. Unlike most restaurants, at the Voyagers the waiters often lend a hand in the kitchen. The service is well informed, but informal.

45½ Mount Auburn Street
Cambridge
354-1718

TURBAN OF SALMON, SOLE AND SPINACH

2 *pounds spinach, washed and stems removed*
2 *tablespoons minced shallots*
¼ *cup butter*
   salt and pepper
   freshly grated nutmeg
   juice of ½ lemon

2 *pounds fresh salmon, boned, skinned and diced*
2 *eggs*
   dash of Tabasco sauce
2 *pints medium cream*
2 *pounds thin, flat fillets of sole*
   lettuce leaves
   lemon wedges
   radishes

1. Preheat oven to 350°.
2. Cook the spinach in boiling, salted water until limp, then drain. Squeeze spinach to wring out all the water and chop finely.
3. Lightly sauté the shallots in butter. Add the spinach, increase heat to high and cook for 3 to 5 minutes to evaporate excess moisture. Season with salt, pepper, nutmeg and lemon juice. Set aside.
4. Purée half the salmon in a food processor and gradually incorporate salt, nutmeg, 1 egg, Tabasco sauce, and 1 pint cream. Process until the mixture is smooth. Repeat the proceedure with the remaining salmon, egg and cream. Combine the salmon mixtures and chill.
5. Bring 3 inches water to a boil in a roasting pan. Generously butter a 6-cup ring mold and line with the sole fillets.
6. Divide the salmon mixture in thirds and spoon the first part into the mold over the sole. Place half the spinach on top of the salmon mixture, add another third of the salmon, the remaining spinach, then the remaining salmon.
7. Cover with buttered waxed paper and a double layer of aluminum foil, set mold in prepared pan of boiling water and bake for 50 to 60 minutes or until the turban feels firm to the touch.
8. Remove from oven, take off foil and allow to cool before unmolding onto a plate somewhat larger than the mold. Drain the turban thoroughly and refrigerate for several hours or overnight.
9. To serve, slice the turban and arrange on plates lined with lettuce leaves. Garnish with lemon wedges and radishes.

CHICKEN AFICIONADO

6 chicken breasts,
   boned and split
6 tablespoons butter
   salt and pepper
1 tablespoon minced shallots
¼ pound Prosciutto ham,
   thinly sliced and slivered

¼ pound mushrooms,
   washed and thinly sliced
½-¾ pound chicken livers,
   each cut in quarters
flour for dusting
pinch of thyme
1 cup Madeira
¼ cup butter

1. Pound the chicken breasts between two pieces of waxed paper until about ⅓-inch thick.
2. Melt the butter in two skillets and heat over a moderate heat until foamy. Add the chicken and sauté both sides for a few minutes until the flesh turns opaque. Remove chicken from pan, season lightly with salt and pepper and transfer to a warm plate.
3. Increase heat to high, adding more butter to pans if necessary, and add the shallots, Prosciutto and mushrooms. Dust the chicken livers with flour and add to pan with salt, pepper and thyme. Sauté until the chicken livers are nicely browned, shaking the pan to prevent sticking.
4. Pour ½ cup Madeira into each pan and deglaze, scraping with a wooden spatula to dissolve congealed meat juices.
5. Transfer the Prosciutto, mushrooms and chicken livers to the chicken platter with a slotted spoon.
6. Combine the juices in one pan and boil until thick and syrupy—approximately ½ cup should remain. Swirl in the remaining butter and pour sauce over the chicken. Serve at once.

We have always felt that the perfect complement to fine food is carefully selected wine. We decant all of our red wines, unless they have no sediment. Our white wines are not stored under refrigeration, but chilled in ice on serving.

HONEY-LEMON CARROTS

3 pounds carrots,
    peeled and cut into sticks
2 bunches scallions, tops
    and roots trimmed

6 tablespoons melted butter
¾ teaspoon salt
3 tablespoons honey
    juice and grated rind
      of 1 lemon

1. Preheat oven to 350°.
2. Immerse the carrots and scallions in boiling, well-salted water and cook until tender crisp. Place in cold water to stop cooking and drain.
3. Combine the remaining ingredients, varying the proportions according to the sweetness of the carrots. Place carrots and scallions in a baking dish, pour the sauce over them and bake for 15 minutes.

To me it is very important to have a connection with the whole food process, from garden, to kitchen, to table. We grow many of our own herbs and vegetables. Our serving people often help out in the kitchen.

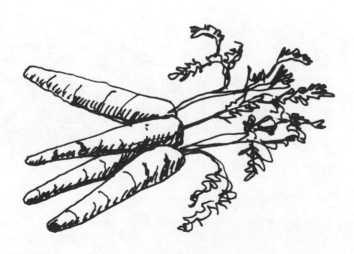

GREEN AND GOLD SQUASH

3 small zucchini
3 small summer or
   yellow squash
salt

1 tablespoon chopped shallots
¼ cup softened butter
   freshly ground black pepper

1. Wash and thinly slice the squash.
2. Bring ½-inch water to a boil in a wide sauté pan with salt and shallots. Add the squash, cover pan and steam for 2 to 3 minutes or until tender.
3. Pour off the water and toss the squash with butter and pepper. Serve at once.

Its hard to know how much to put into a recipe. You want to give people plenty of freedom to cook to their own taste.

My advice to the neophyte is this: you can do a lot more than you think you can, if only you can survive the first two months in the restaurant.

STRAWBERRIES CASSIS

1 cup *CRÈME FRAÎCHE*
¾ cup *heavy cream,*
   stiffly whipped
¼ cup *crème de cassis*
   splash of port wine
   squeeze of lemon juice

sugar to taste
2 quarts *fresh ripe straw-*
   berries, washed and hulled
1 cup *seedless grapes*
3 tablespoons *shelled,*
   chopped pistachio nuts

1. Combine Crème Fraîche, whipped cream, crème de cassis, port, lemon juice and sugar, adjusting the sweetness or tartness to suit the berries.

2. Arrange the berries and grapes in a glass bowl and pour the sauce over them, letting some of the bright red peek out. Garnish with chopped pistachio nuts for serving.

Note: Crème de cassis is a liqueur made from black currants. It is available in specialty spirit shops.

CRÈME FRAÎCHE

1 quart *heavy cream*

1 pint *buttermilk*
   or sour cream

Combine the cream and buttermilk and heat to tepid. Cover and let stand in a warm place overnight. When the mixture is thick and sourish, the Crème Fraîche is ready.

This recipe produces a good approximation of the thick, sourish cream used by the French.

We try to emphasize knowledge, rather than formality, in our service.

As a self-taught cook, I have much more freedom than someone who was trained at cooking school. I haven't been told what I must or must not do.

ZACHARY'S

Dinner for Six

Casserole Rockefeller

Green Bean Salad

Truite à la Muscovite

Pommes Persil

Gâteau Colonnade

Wines:

*With the Scallops and Trout—Corton-Charlemagne
(Louis Latour) 1973*

With the Dessert—Château d'Yquem 1971

Victor Pap, Chef

Not long after the opening of the Colonade Hotel a few blocks west of Copley Square, its luxury restaurant, Zachary's had won national acclaim for its Continental cuisine and formal French service. Recipient of a distinguished restaurant award from United Airline's *Mainliner* magazine, Zachary's has hosted dinners for prestigious gourmet societies such as the Chaîne de Rôtisseurs and Les Amis de'Escoffier. Colonnade guests have included Beverly Sills, Ryan O'Neal, Golda Meir and former President Ford.

It is easy to see why the Colonnade prides itself on Zachary's unique setting. The dining room is a facsimile of the famous French cruise ship *Degrasse*, which plied the seas in the 1920's and 30's. Antique French chrome mirrors and custom fabrics adorn the walls of the 115-seat dining area. Zachary's guests dine on fine Rosenthal china imported from Germany.

Zachary's bill of fare reflects the international background of Executive Chef Victor Pap. Born in Hungary, he trained in Austria, Italy and Germany, before coming to Boston. A veteran at Zachary's, Pap oversees thirteen chefs and a four-man pastry team who help him add sixty new dishes to Zachary's menu each year.

One evening a gentleman asked the maître d' to help him surprise a lady friend. The mustachioed maître d' readily obliged by placing a diamond ring inside a whipped-cream pastry.

120 Huntington Avenue
424-7000

CASSEROLE ROCKEFELLER

½ cup butter
3 pounds spinach, washed
   and stems removed
¼ cup Pernod

6 tablespoons WHITE SAUCE
  salt and pepper
1½ pounds Bay or
   Cape scallops
1 cup dried bread crumbs

1. Preheat oven to 500°.
2. Melt 3 tablespoons butter in a large sauté pan and cook the spinach with Pernod. Once the leaves wilt, increase heat to evaporate excess moisture. Remove from heat and set aside.
3. Chop spinach coarsely, stir in the White Sauce and correct the seasoning.
4. Butter six small ramekins or scallop shells and divide the mixture among them.
5. Season the scallops with salt and pepper and dredge in bread crumbs, shaking off excess. Place on top of spinach.
6. Dot with the remaining butter and bake until golden brown— approximately 6 to 8 minutes. Serve immediately.

WHITE SAUCE

2 teaspoons butter
2 teaspoons flour

⅓ cup milk
  grating of fresh nutmeg
  salt and pepper

Melt the butter in a small saucepan and whisk in the flour. Cook for 3 minutes, but do not let brown. Gradually whisk in the milk and simmer for 3 more minutes. Season to taste before using.

Why do we change our menu only once a year? I can only quote from Goethe: "Art is long; life, short." At Zachary's we prepare cuisine which is a work of art.

GREEN BEAN SALAD

1½ pounds green beans,
   washed, snapped and
   sliced on the diagonal
⅓ cup red wine vinegar
3 tablespoons olive oil

1 small onion, finely chopped
½ teaspoon salt
¼ teaspoon freshly ground
   black pepper
   lettuce leaves
   diced pimiento

1. Immerse the green beans in a large pot of boiling, salted water and cook for 3 to 4 minutes or until tender crisp. Drain.
2. Combine the vinegar, oil, onion, salt and pepper and add the hot green beans. Chill for at least 1 hour.
3. Arrange lettuce leaves on six chilled salad plates. Drain green beans and pile in the center. Garnish with diced pimiento before serving.

Think of Zachary's as Symphony Hall and the chef as the composer. The maître d' plays the role of the conductor, ensuring that the guests are served the food properly and that the performance unfolds in the dining room exactly as it was conceived by the chef in the kitchen.

TRUITE À LA MUSCOVITE

6 (10-ounce) trout
¾ cup chopped onion
6 tablespoons butter
3 tablespoons flour
9 ounces crab meat, flaked
1½ tablespoons Cognac
1½ tablespoons black caviar
    salt and pepper

2 teaspoons finely
    chopped parsley
¼ teaspoon chervil
1 egg plus 1 yolk, beaten
    flour for dredging
½ cup olive oil
    CAVIAR SAUCE
    parsley sprigs
    lemon wedges

1. Preheat oven to 350°.
2. Clean trout through the gills and remove backbones, leaving the heads and tails intact (or have your fishmonger do it). Rinse and pat dry.
3. Briskly sauté onion in butter for 3 minutes or until golden. Stir in the flour and cook for 1 minute. Add the crab meat, Cognac, caviar, parsley, chervil, salt and pepper. Cook to heat the mixture through. Stir in the egg and the yolk and cook 1 minute. Remove from heat and let cool.
4. Season the trout cavities with salt and pepper. Spread the trout open, divide the stuffing evenly among the cavities and press closed.
5. Dredge trout in flour, shaking off excess, and sauté over high heat in a large skillet in olive oil for 2 minutes per side.
6. Transfer to an oven-proof platter and bake for 12 t 15 minutes. Arrange on a serving platter and spoon the Caviar Sauce on top. Garnish with parsley sprigs and lemon wedges for serving.

CAVIAR SAUCE

6 tablespoons clarified butter
6 tablespoons flour
2¼ cups FISH STOCK (see index)
   or bottled clam juice
½ cup sour cream

¼ cup dry white wine
pinch of thyme
salt and pepper
3 tablespoons caviar
1½ tablespoons butter

1. Melt butter in a saucepan and whisk in the flour. Cook for 3 minutes or until golden. Gradually whisk in the Fish Stock and simmer, stirring for 5 minutes. Add sour cream, wine and seasonings and simmer for 5 more minutes.

2. Strain sauce and gently stir in the caviar. Dot with butter to prevent a skin from forming. Keep warm.

Perfection requires enormous planning and practice. Great dishes are not born overnight.

POMMES PERSIL

6 boiling potatoes,
   peeled and quartered

3 tablespoons butter
3 tablespoons finely
   chopped parsley

Place the potatoes in a large pot with ½-inch salted water. Bring to a boil, cover pan and steam potatoes 25 minutes or until tender. Place in a serving dish and toss with butter and parsley.

GÂTEAU COLONNADE

1 cup sugar
⅓ cup cocoa
¾ cup cake flour
1 cup milk
½ cup unsalted butter
    at room temperature

1 teaspoon baking powder
1 teaspoon baking soda
6 eggs
CHOCOLATE MINT
    FROSTING

1. Preheat oven to 350°.
2. Grease and lightly flour 3 (8-inch) cake pans and line the bottoms with waxed paper.
3. Combine the sugar, cocoa, flour and ⅓ cup milk in the bowl of a mixer. Beat in the butter, baking powder and baking soda, mixing at medium speed for 5 minutes.
4. Beat in 3 eggs and 3 tablespoons milk. Continue mixing for 2 to 3 minutes, scraping sides and bottom of bowl frequently. Add the remaining eggs and milk. Beat at high speed for 1 minute.
5. Pour batter into prepared pans and bake for 20 minutes or until the tops spring back when pressed gently. Cool and turn out onto a wire rack. Be sure to remove the waxed paper.
6. Ice each cake with Chocolate Mint Frosting and stack the layers. Smooth the icing on top with a spatula. This cake serves 12 to 14.

CHOCOLATE MINT FROSTING

¼ cup milk
8 ounces unsweetened
    chocolate
¾ cup confectioners' sugar

¼ cup white corn syrup
2 tablespoons crème
    de menthe

Combine milk, chocolate, sugar and corn syrup in a saucepan and bring barely to a boil, stirring constantly. Cool and stir in the liqueur.

The Gâteau Colonnade is probably our most famous dessert. The critics say it's the best chocolate cake in Boston.

RECIPE INDEX

RECIPE INDEX

RECIPE INDEX

ABOUT THE AUTHOR

Steven Raichlen was born in Nagoya, Japan, in 1953. ("I didn't eat *sushi* until I was 20, however.") After a brief attempt at a career as a rock musican, he attended Reed College in Portland, Oregon, where he majored in French literature. While at Reed, Steve worked part-time at Otto's, a delicatessen that sold fine wine and manufactured its own sausage. During his senior year, Steve applied for a fellowship from the Thomas J. Watson Foundation. Much to his surprise, he received $7000 from the foundation for a one year study of medieval cooking in Europe. His research took him to Germany, Austria, Hungary, France, England, Italy, and Greece, where he pored over dusty old cookbooks. Steve also spent six months in Paris at the Cordon Bleu and La Varenne cooking schools where he became hooked on classical and contemporary French cuisine. He later became U.S. program co-ordinator for La Varenne, accompanying French chefs teaching in the U.S.

His writing career began in Boston in 1977, when he translated the memoirs of Claude Terrail, owner of the prestigious Tour d'Argent restaurant of Paris. He then wrote freelance articles for the Real Paper, the Phoenix, the Globe, the Washington Post, and the Christian Science Moniter. He was also a contributing editor of the *Book of Lists*, the *People's Almanac*, and Anne Willan's *Paris Kitchen*. His first book, *Dining In–Boston* appeared in 1980. More recently, Steve edited the *Left Bank Cookbook* by Vail, Colorado restaurateur Luc Meyer, the preface of which was written by President Ford. His newest book, *Steven Raichlen's Guide to Boston Restaurants*, is due to be published by the Stephan Green Press this fall.

He is also the restaurant critic and food and wine columnist for Boston Magazine. The questions he is most frequently asked as a restaurant critic are "What's your favorite restaurant?" and "How do you stay so slim?" (He weighs 125 pounds.) "I have written this book to answer the former; the latter remains a trade secret."

DINING IN–THE GREAT CITIES
A Collection of Gourmet Recipes from the Finest Chefs in the Country

Each book contains gourmet recipes for complete meals from the chefs of 21 great restaurants.

____ *Dining In–Baltimore* $7.95	____ *Dining In–Monterey Peninsula* $7.95
____ *Dining In–Boston (Revised)* 8.95	____ *Dining In–Philadelphia* 8.95
____ *Dining In–Chicago, Vol. II* 8.95	____ *Dining In–Phoenix* 8.95
____ *Dining In–Chicago, Vol. III* 8.95	____ *Dining In–Pittsburgh (Revised)* 7.95
____ *Dining In–Cleveland* 8.95	____ *Dining In–Portland* 7.95
____ *Dining In–Dallas (Revised)* 8.95	____ *Dining In–St. Louis* 7.95
____ *Dining In–Denver* 7.95	____ *Dining In–San Francisco, Vol. II (Spring '83)* 8.95
____ *Dining In–Hawaii* 8.95	____ *Dining In–Seattle, Vol. III* 8.95
____ *Dining In–Houston, Vol. II* 7.95	____ *Dining In–Sun Valley* 7.95
____ *Dining In–Kansas City (Revised)* 8.95	____ *Dining In–Toronto* 8.95
____ *Dining In–Los Angeles (Revised)* 8.95	____ *Dining In–Vail* 8.95
____ *Dining In–Manhattan* 8.95	____ *Dining In–Vancouver, B.C.* 8.95
____ *Dining In–Milwaukee* 8.95	____ *Dining In–Washington, D.C.* 8.95
____ *Dining In–Minneapolis/St. Paul, Vol. II* . 8.95	

☐ Check (✔) here is you would like to have a different Dining In–Cookbook sent to you once a month. Payable by MasterCard or VISA. Returnable if not satisfied.

Please include $1.00 postage and handling for each book.

☐ Payment enclosed $ _____ (total amount)

☐ Charge to:

VISA # _____ Exp. Date _____

MasterCard # _____ Exp. Date _____

Signature _____

Name _____

Address _____

City _____ State _____ Zip _____

SHIP TO (if other than name and address above):

Name _____

Address _____

City _____ State _____ Zip _____

PEANUT BUTTER PUBLISHING
2445 76th Avenue S.E. ▪ Mercer Island, WA 98040 ▪ (206) 236-1982

WITHDRAWN
No longer the property of the
Boston Public Library.
Sale of this material benefited the Library.